Henry Joy McCracken

HISTORICAL ASSOCIATION OF IRELAND

LIFE AND TIMES

NEW SERIES

General Editor: Ciaran Brady

Henry Joy McCracken

JIM SMYTH

✦

Published on behalf of
the Historical Association of Ireland
by

UNIVERSITY COLLEGE DUBLIN PRESS
Preas Choláiste Ollscoile Bhaile Átha Cliath
2020

This first edition published 2020 in collaboration with the
Historical Association of Ireland by
University College Dublin Press

ISBN 978-1-910820-52-0
ISSN 2009-1397

University College Dublin Press
UCD Humanities Institute
Dublin 4, Ireland
www.ucdpress.ie

Cataloguing in Publication data available from the British Library

Typeset in Scotland in Ehrhardt by Ryan Shiels
Text design by Lyn Davies
Printed in Dublin on acid-free paper by
SPRINT-Print, Rathcoole, County Dublin, Ireland

CONTENTS

FOREWORD

Originally conceived over a decade ago to place the lives of leading figures in Irish history against the background of new research on the problems and conditions of their times and modern assessments of their historical significance, the Historical Association of Ireland Life and Times series enjoyed remarkable popularity and success. A second series has now been planned in association with UCD Press in a new format and with fuller scholarly apparatus. Encouraged by the reception given to the earlier series, the volumes in the new series will be expressly designed to be of particular help to students preparing for the Leaving Certificate, for GCE Advanced Level and for undergraduate history courses, as well as appealing to the happily insatiable appetite for new views of Irish history among the general public.

CIARAN BRADY
Historical Association of Ireland

This little book is dedicated to the memory of Brendan Bradshaw,
Saoí Séimh

*

ACKNOWLEDGEMENTS

I wish to thank the general editor of this series, Ciaran Brady, for suggesting that I introduce a brief life of Henry Joy McCracken into the gloriously mixed company on its list; Brendan MacSuibhne for reading, and commenting upon a draft of the text; and Stephen Smyth for the opportunity of writing some of it up in the hills of Donegal. My gratitude also to friends and colleagues in the History Department, and the Keough-Naughton Institute for Irish Studies, in the University of Notre Dame: Chris Fox, Patrick Griffin, John McGreevy, and Peter McQuillan.

JIM SMYTH
January 2020

ABBREVIATIONS

BNL	*Belfast News-Letter*
LHL	Linen Hall Library
PRONI	Public Record Office, Northern Ireland.

CHRONOLOGY OF McCRACKEN'S LIFE AND TIMES

1767
31 August Henry Joy McCracken born, High St, Belfast.

5th Earl of Donegal begins the re-leasing of his many Belfast properties, prompting urban renewal and growth over the coming decades.

1776
4 July American Declaration of Independence.

1778
17 March The first company of Belfast Volunteers founded in the home of Robert Joy (Henry Joy's uncle).

1779
4 November Volunteer parade in College Green demands 'Free Trade'.

1782
15 February Volunteer Convention in Dungannon demands legislative independence and a relaxation of the penal laws.

16 April–17 May The repeal of the Declaratory Act, and the amendment of 'Poynings' Law' – 'the Constitution of 1782'.

1789
14 July The Fall of the Bastille, Paris.

1790
1 November Edmund Burke's *Reflections on the Revolution in France* is published.

1791

13 March publication of Thomas Paine's *Rights of Man,* part one.

14 July The Volunteers celebrate the second anniversary of the Fall of the Bastille in Belfast and Dublin.

c.22 August publication of Theobald Wolfe Tone's *An Argument on Behalf of the Catholics of Ireland.*

14 October The Society of United Irishmen founded in Belfast.

9 November founding of the Dublin Society of United Irishmen.

1792

4 January First printing of the United Irish paper, *The Northern Star,* Belfast.

18 April Catholic Relief Act.

11–14 July Irish Harpers festival, Belfast.

14 July Volunteer celebrations on the third anniversary of the fall of the Bastille.

3–5 December Catholic Convention, Tailors' Hall, Back Lane, Dublin.

1793

21 January Execution of Louis XVI in Paris.

1 February France declares war on Great Britain.

March Henry Joy takes oath in the 'underground' United Irishmen.

9 April Catholic Relief Act.

22 April Henry Joy confronts the garrison commander on the street, during a military riot in Belfast.

1794

23 May Suppression of the Dublin Society of United Irishmen.

1795

4 January–23 February Lord lieutenancy of Earl Fitzwilliam.

Late May On Cave Hill, overlooking Belfast Lough, Henry Joy, Wolfe Tone and others take 'a solemn obligation ... never to desist in our efforts until we have subverted the authority of England over our country and asserted our independence'.

June Henry Joy joins Masonic Lodge, 783, and is appointed Deputy Commander of the County Antrim Defenders.

21 September Battle of the Diamond, Loughgall, County Armagh. Formation of the Orange Order.

1796

24 March Insurrection Act.

16 September Leading United Irishmen arrested in Belfast and Lisburn and held without trial as state prisoners.

10 October Henry Joy arrested and incarcerated in Kilmainham Gaol as a state prisoner.

26 October Suspension of Habeus Corpus.

22–7 December Part of a French Invasion fleet reaches Bantry Bay, County Cork, but is thwarted by bad weather.

1797

13 March General Lake's Proclamation of Ulster. General disarming commences.

19 May Monaghan Militia destroy the printing presses of *The Northern Star*.

14 October William Orr hanged near Carrickfergus, County Antrim.

November Publication of Edward Bunting's *A General Collection of the Ancient Irish Music*.

9 December Henry Joy bailed out of prison on grounds of ill health.

1798

12 March Arrest of majority of members of the United Irish Leinster Directory, in the home of Oliver Bond, Dublin.

30 March Ireland proclaimed to be in a state of rebellion.

19 May Lord Edward captured and fatally wounded (dies 4 June).

23 May Rebellion begins in Leinster.

30 May Insurgents occupy Wexford Town.

5 June The Battle of New Ross, County Wexford.

6 June Henry Joy, Commander in Chief, 'Army of Ulster', issues general orders to march on Antrim Town.

7 June The Battle of Antrim.

13 June The Battle of Ballynahinch.

21 June The Wexford Rebellion is crushed at Vinegar Hill, near Enniscorthy.

7 July Henry Joy arrested on the Carrickfergus road.

17 July Henry Joy court-martialled and hanged in Corn Market, Belfast.

Introduction
Ireland in the Age of Revolution

As in most of Europe, late eighteenth-century Irish politics and society were affected profoundly by the American and French revolutions. The first led to the overthrow of British imperial rule, the second to the overturning of monarchy and to the destruction of the aristocratic *ancien regime*. The fierce conflict in Ireland in the 1790s led to none of these things, for this was also the age of counter-revolution. Nonetheless, the failed attempt by the United Irish movement to found an independent republic by force of arms, which culminated in the Great Rebellion of 1798, is by any standard a momentous and consequential historical event.

The political structures of eighteenth-century Ireland were confessional – a Protestant state entrenched behind palisades of penal laws, ratified the expropriation of Catholic land, and excluded Catholics from public office. As the hardline Protestant politician John Fitzgibbon, 1st earl of Clare, freely admitted, 'the act by which most of us hold our estates was an act of violence'. He referred to the Williamite settlement (1691) and to the corpus of anti-popery legislation that followed, and pointed out that the security of those estates rested ultimately in 'dependence upon the crown of England'.[1] In September 1792 Dublin Corporation issued a declaration defining 'Protestant ascendancy' as: 'a Protestant king of

Ireland, a Protestant hierarchy, Protestant electors and government – the benches of justice – the army and the revenue – through all their branches and details, Protestant'. And the Dublin Corporation understood as well as Fitzgibbon that their minority lock on power depended upon the 'connection with the Protestant realm of England'.[2]

The Corporation's declaration responded to a campaign for relief from penal laws, mounted by the Catholic Committee, revived and emboldened by the democratic spirit (or 'contagion' as conservatives, including Catholic bishops, preferred) of the French Revolution. And that campaign seemed uniquely threatening to the ascendancy because of the support it enjoyed from of a section of Irish Protestants-without-a-hierarchy: the Presbyterians, or dissenters, of Ulster. Historically, tensions had subsisted between the Presbyterians concentrated in the north east, and the established Church. Now, in October 1791 some of the former founded the Society of United Irishmen in Belfast, followed a few weeks later by a Dublin Society, composed near equally of Catholic activists and the more radically disposed Protestants (mainly) of the Church of Ireland. Their primary objective was parliamentary reform, but they swiftly embraced Catholic relief as well.

The Catholics did wring concessions out of the parliament, which passed relief acts in 1792 and 1793. United Irish demands for reform were however rejected. Indeed, the space for political agitation shrank dramatically. As Britain went to war against revolutionary France, its ascendancy clients in Dublin Castle began to crack down on 'disaffection'. During the course of the 1793 anti-militia riots the levels of both state and popular violence crossed new thresholds for eighteenth-century Ireland.[3] Much worse would follow. When the pathways to political reform began to shut down, and their organisation was effectively proscribed, the United Irishmen went 'underground'. As early as 1791 Theobald Wolfe Tone, a founding member, had privately expressed a preference for Ireland separating from England; by mid-decade an Irish Republic, to be established with the military assistance of revolutionary France, had become United Irish policy.

Thanks not least to Tone's skilled lobbying in the Parisian corridors of power, in December 1796 a French invasionary force set sail for Ireland. Three ships made it into Bantry Bay, but the rest were scattered in the Atlantic by the proverbial 'Protestant wind'. England had had its closest call since the Spanish Armada, and her Irish garrison duly responded to the now demonstrable French threat by ratcheting up its campaign of repression. House-burnings, arms searches, floggings, and wholesale arrests – the so-called 'dragooning of Ulster' – were conducted under the command of General Lake. Many of the United Irish leadership in Belfast, including Henry Joy McCracken, were already state prisoners, and this, combined with the impact of the counter-insurgency, meant that during 1797 the revolutionary initiative shifted south to Dublin.

One of the paradoxes of the 1790s is that there is a mismatch of sorts between the map of the rebellion and the geography of political activity that preceded it. In terms of scale events in those veritable powerhouses of politicisation, east Ulster and Dublin, are not comparable to the rebellion in Wexford and south Wicklow. Whereas the casualties at the battle of Antrim on 7 June 1798 can be measured in hundreds, the number of dead at the battle of New Ross just two days before runs into the thousands.[4] The lesser scale notwithstanding, the fighting in Antrim and Down mattered because in contrast to the mainly Catholic insurgents in Wexford, and later in the summer when a small French force did manage to land in Mayo and Longford, most of the northern rebels were

Presbyterian. That 'turn-out' as the locals called it, lent ballast to Wolfe Tone's badly-battered republican credo of uniting Protestant, Catholic, and dissenter under the common name of Irishman; and the turn-out might well not have happened at all but for the decisive actions of one man – Henry Joy McCracken.

CHAPTER ONE

Belfast

The story of Henry Joy McCracken ends where it began, in the town of Belfast. As he stood upon the gallows in Cornmarket on 17 July 1798 he had a clear view of High Street where he was born, where the Joy and McCracken families once lived as near neighbours, and along which on 14 July 1792 he marched in Volunteer uniform to celebrate the third anniversary of the fall of the Bastille. The Volunteers, a citizen army, originated with the First Belfast Company started in 1778 by Henry's uncle Robert Joy, and joined early on by his brothers Francis and William McCracken. In the terse account of his execution provided by the *Belfast News-Letter* (no longer the voice of Whig moderation, founded in 1737 by his grandfather Francis Joy): 'at five o'clock the prisoner was brought out from the artillery barracks to the place of execution. Having been attended in prison by a clergyman, he was only a few minutes from the time he came out, till he was launched into eternity. After hanging one hour his body was given to his friends.'[1] He had, in his own words, 'done his duty'. He was just short of 31 years old.

The story of Henry Joy's life is fused with the history and environs of eighteenth-century Belfast. After Dublin and Cork, Belfast was the third largest port in Ireland: small, compact, and expanding; charged with commercial, religious, and intellectual energy; blasted by John Milton in 1649 as 'a barbarous nook . . .

whose obscurity till now never came to our hearing'. By Henry Joy's time Belfast was dubbed by its admirers 'the Athens of the North'. The name derives from the Irish, *Béal Feirste*, which means roughly the mouth of (or approach to) the sandbank (or crossing), the place where the river Farset flows into the river Lagan, and on into what would become known as Belfast Lough. Although the spelling 'Belfast' did not stabilise formally until the Ordnance Survey mapping of Ireland (1825–46), Garrett Og Fitzgerald refers to Belfast – the site of a several times sacked (minor) Norman castle – as early as 1523. Later in the sixteenth century, however, it is also rendered Belfaste and Bellfest. In 1603 the crown granted Sir Arthur Chichester 'the castle of Bealfaste or Belfast'. The United Irishman Theobald Wolfe Tone in 1791 made Swiftian allusions to Blefuscu; but by then, and long before the imprimatur accorded by the Ordnance Survey, the spelling had settled and there was a 54-year-old newspaper title to prove it.[2]

Belfast is maritime. In a 1786 painting, ships' masts are visible on the skyline, closing the vista to the High Street. The early seventeenth-century settlement grew up on the west bank of the river Lagan, alongside the castle. However, it is the basalt-capped mountain range, rising at its height to 1,600 feet above sea level, predominately the Black Mountain to the west and north stretching on to Cave Hill and overlooking the lough which, in the words of one of the first historians of that parish, George Benn, 'bestow uncommon grandeur and beauty on the general appearance of the town'[3.] Henry Joy and his fellow northerners shared a strong attachment to the place where he was born and where he was killed. To celebrate the victory of the two popular Whig candidates for County Antrim in the 1790 general election – the 93-year old Francis Joy had travelled from his home in Randalstown to Carrickfergus to cast his vote – the citizens of Belfast lit two bonfires, one in the market place and a second on 'the romantic summit of Cave Hill . . . to the view of several adjoining counties'.[4] Thomas Russell, Henry Joy's exact contemporary, comrade in arms, and Cork man gone native, recalled a day in June 1791 on Cave Hill with his beloved, Eliza Goddard, as the happiest of his life.[5] More well-known, indeed an iconic moment in Irish republican history, is the excursion by Russell, McCracken, Samuel Neilson, Wolfe Tone and others in May 1795. Tone, taking leave of his Belfast friends before sailing for America and into political exile, gathered with them at MacArt's Fort, Cave Hill, where they 'took a solemn obligation . . . never to desist in our efforts until we have subverted the authority of England over our country and asserted our independence.'[6] Aptly enough in his final days 'on the run' Henry Joy went to ground in the Belfast mountains.

The political landscape and human geography of late eighteenth-century Belfast originates in the remaking of Ulster after 1603 and were shaped by the fortunes of Sir Arthur Chichester and his dynasty – the ships' masts in the 1786 painting of the High Street rise from Hanover and Chichester Quays. Governor of Carrickfergus and Clandeboye since 1599, a seasoned Elizabethan 'Captain', and chief architect of the scorched earth subjugation of the O'Neill rebellion in Ulster, in 1603 Chichester was rewarded for his services to the crown by grants of land in upper Clandeboye (loosely south County Antrim) including the castle in Belfast with its 'Appurtenants and Hereditaments, Spiritual and Temporal'. He assumed office as Lord Deputy of Ireland in 1605, and five years later received the title Baron Chichester of Belfast. In 1613 the town was incorporated, but that new status did not denote its significance as an emerging port or budding urban hub; rather the new corporation borough joined 39 other boroughs, created across plantation Ulster at the time, each enfranchised in various ways to elect two (invariably Protestant) representatives to a parliament in which Old English Catholics still, just about, held a majority. The local results of incorporation were lasting and consequential nonetheless.

By Royal Charter, municipal governance devolved to the Sovereign, Free Burgesses, and Commonality; 12 burgesses selected one of their number as Sovereign, and they in turn were – effectively – appointed for life, by the earl of Chichester (from 1647 Earl, and from 1791, Marquess of Donegall). In Dublin, it is true, the Board of Aldermen elected the Lord Mayor; however, Dublin boasted a common council, representing the trades guilds whose members were, unlike Belfast's 'Freemen', entitled to vote in parliamentary elections. In contrast Belfast's two MPs were returned by 13 men answerable only to their patron. Electoral anomalies luxuriated of course in a franchise ecosystem based on different gradations of property qualification and *ancien regime* privilege developed *ad hoc*– its admirers insisted 'organically' – over several centuries. Yet the Belfast dispensation still presents a glaring example of the – in this case wholly intentional – misalignment of parliamentary constituency to local civil society. Most of the respectable citizenry, merchants and manufacturers, men of property, Presbyterian probity, and education, were excluded from the corporation, and therefore denied the right to vote on grounds of religious confession, not real estate. That is why the comparatively 'open' popularly contested, County Antrim elections could generate such formidable political mobilisation and excitement.

The Sacramental Test Act of 1704, debarring Protestant dissenters from public office, formalised divisions between manse and Church, or more broadly, between Scots and English settlers, which fissured the Ulster plantation from the start. Chichester, who 'had no special affection for Scotsmen, high or low, gentle or simple',[7] recruited tenants to his estates in Malone –along the Lagan valley from the castle, and in the area around Carrickfergus – from his native Devonshire; but the English colonists were soon out-numbered by lowland Scots. The larger-scale Scottish migration resulted from the accession of James VI of Scotland to the English throne, geography, chance, and chicanery. In 1603, after a brawl between some of his men and the soldiery in Carrickfergus, Conn O'Neill, Lord of Clandeboye, was jailed for rebellion, and then 'rescued' by an Ayrshire laird, Hugh Montgomery. Montgomery offered to obtain a pardon for O'Neill from the new king in exchange for half of his estates. In the event, another Scottish courtier, Sir James Hamilton, persuaded the king to divide the lordship three ways. Settlers from nearby south-west Scotland began arriving in numbers in north County Down in 1606 three years before the commencement of the Ulster Plantation proper (in which Antrim and Down were not included). These were the people, and their descendants, who stamped their distinctive character on the town on the other side of the river Lagan, and during the seventeenth century that regional character – or iden-tity – was primarily Presbyterian.

Edward Brice enters the record in 1613 as Ireland's first Presbyterian minister, but that bare fact is on its own misleading. Presbyterianism is a form of Church polity, as well as a body of doctrine and liturgical practice. Ministers are 'called' by congrega-tions, which they serve in conjunction with elected lay elders; congregations are represented collectively at synod, and in Scotland in this period by General Assembly, the moderatorship of which rotates annually, also by election. The moral rectitude of clergy and laity alike is policed by courts of kirk session. Put negatively, Presbyters rejected the authority of bishops – prelacy or episco-pacy – and the more militant (or purist) among them also rejected any 'Erastian' intervention by the temporal state in Church affairs. But in 1613 Brice left one episcopal jurisdiction, that of the Church of Scotland, and entered another, that of the Church of

Ireland. In fact, the Bishop of Down and Connor assigned the cure
of Ballygarry, County Antrim to Brice. Ulster and Scotland at this
time had 'Presbyterian' ministers and congregations absent a
Presbyterian Church.

As John Milton's rebuke to 'the blockish presbyters of Clandeboye'
indicates, the politics of Presbyterianism in seventeenth-century
Ulster only make sense within a three kingdoms framework. 'The
divisions which from time to time occurred in the Kirk of Scotland'
observed A. T. Q. Stewart, 'tended, like fault lines in the geological
structure, to reappear on the Ulster side of the North Channel.'[8]
Ultimately, however, all were subject to ecclesiastical policy made
in London, with momentous consequences for Presbyterians on
both sides of the water. In the 1630s ministers like Brice were
'silenced' or expelled from their livings as Archbishop William
Laud attempted to impose conformity to the established Church
across the three kingdoms. The Revd Robert Blair, formerly
professor in the University of Glasgow, who had left Scotland to
evade the impositions of prelacy now went into a sort of reverse
exile. Blair was one of a number of Ulster ministers at the 1638
General Assembly in Edinburgh, which promulgated the National
Covenant and abolished episcopacy. The covenanting movement
denotated a political crisis involving the Lord Deputy of Ireland,
and close ally of Laud, Sir Thomas Wentworth, coercing the inhabitants of east Ulster into swearing a 'Black Oath' renouncing
the covenant, and in October 1641 a rebellion by the Catholic, native
Irish that threatened to sweep the plantation into the sea. In April
1642, a Scots army coming to the relief of their brethren, landed at
Carrickfergus, bringing with it the covenant, chaplains, and kirk
sessions. It is at this point that the history of the Presbyterian
Church in Ireland begins.

The intricate diplomatic conduct of the wars of the three
kingdoms shaped the Presbyterian experience for generations to

come. First, in 1643 the Scots made a military pact with the English parliament against the King's forces, *The Solemn League and Covenant*, committing both parties to a Presbyterian settlement. And second, the following year English 'Puritans' and the Scots negotiated a supposedly prescriptive formulae, *The Westminster Confession of Faith*. In one of the many ironies in a decade of shifting, uneasy, unlikely, and unnatural, alliances, in 1649 the Belfast Presbytery issued its *Necessary Representation*, condemning the English parliament for executing Charles I, and aligning itself thereby with royalist and Irish Catholic Confederate forces still in arms. The company they were now keeping did not escape the attention of parliament's Latin Secretary John Milton.

Of course neither the Commonwealth of the 1650s nor the restored monarchy of Charles II after 1660 upheld the covenants.[9] In Ulster the returning bishops expelled Presbyterian ministers from their livings *en masse*. Scotland witnessed armed conflict and mass imprisonment, escalating by the 1680s into a campaign of persecution known in Covenanter lore as 'the Killing Times'. Refugees, among them ancestors of Henry Joy's lieutenant James 'Jemmy' Hope, fled the south west Covenanter heartlands of Aryshire and Galloway for the comparative safety of Antrim and Down. In Ireland, however, intra-protestant antipathies swiftly shrank into insignificance as churchman and presbyter closed ranks in the face of James VII and II's Lord Deputy, Richard Talbot, earl of Tyrconnell's drive to re-Catholicise the political nation. For example, Belfast's remodelled borough charter installed a Catholic majority among the burgesses, who duly returned Daniel O'Neale (one of the too many Os and Macs about which King James muttered) and Marcus Talbot to the 1689 parliament.

William III and his army camped at Belfast on their way to the Battle of the Boyne in July 1690, and tradition records that the 'long bridge'– constructed between 1682 and 1688, and crossing

the Lagan on the County Down side at Ballymccarrett – was
structurally impaired by the transportation over it of the Duke of
Schomberg's cannon, as a result of which, two years later, some of
its arches collapsed.[10] Throughout the eighteenth century the toast
to the Glorious and Immortal memory of William of Orange
celebrated the British kingdoms deliverance from 'popery, brass
money, and wooden shoes', and the establishment of 'freedom,
religion, and laws'. William increased the *regium donum*, a crown
stipend for Presbyterian ministers, and perhaps more important, a
token of official legitimacy. From 1690 an Ulster Synod now elected
a moderator on the Scottish model. And reinforcing institutional
development, the northeast during the following decade hosted
the biggest influx of lowland-Scots immigrants since the original
plantation. In 1696 the young, Scotophobic and dissenter-allergic
Jonathan Swift, found his first clerical posting, to the prebendary
of Kilroot, near Carrickfergus, a lonely and uncongenial station.[11]

Upon the succession of the High Church Queen Anne in 1702,
Daniel Defoe published a pamphlet entitled *The Shortest Way with
the Dissenters*, signalling the reversal of religious toleration (for
protestant nonconformists like himself) that had characterised
William's reign. In Ireland the introduction of a religious test in
1704 purged local government, including (three years later) Belfast
corporation of Presbyterians, and by 1710 the impact in Ireland of
the Tory revanche in England is marked by, among other initia-
tives, the aggressive churchmanship of Swift's friend, the vicar of
Belfast, William Tisdall. Tisdall demanded 'House Money', a
form of tithe, which local Presbyterians contested, and engaged in
polemic, *A Sample of True-Blew Presbyterian Loyalty*, answered
from Glasgow by John MacBride's, *Sample of Jet-Black Prelatic
Calumny*. *Regium donum* was suspended in 1713. For rather different
reasons then, the memory of Queen Anne persisted in the Ulster
Presbyterian imagination almost as vividly as that of King William.

A century after 1714 the constitutionalist Whig, Henry Joy Jnr (a cousin of Henry Joy McCracken) comments that upon news of her death 'as the vulgar saying was "the cork flew out of the brandy bottle"'.[12]

With good reason protestant dissenters welcomed the Hanoverian Succession, and for two generations remained bottom-line supporters of the regime, if not all of its policies or government personnel. Belatedly, the Dublin parliament passed a Toleration Act in 1719, but the Test Act remained on the statute books until 1780. Effectively left to their own devices, Ulster's Presbyterians turned to the question of subscription to *The Westminster Confession of Faith*. To its defenders *The Westminster Confession* set a necessary standard for orthodoxy; non-subscribers argued the sufficiency of scripture, and the inviolability of individual judgement and conscience *contra* man-made formulae. In 1719 the year when the subscription controversy blew up in London, the Revd John Abernathy preached (a later published) sermon in Belfast, 'Religious obedience founded on personal persuasion'. In 1721 Abernathy and 11 others, refusing to subscribe, seceded from the Synod of Ulster and founded the Antrim Presbytery. They went by the name of 'New Light'.[13] With their insistence upon rational inquiry and aura of eighteenth-century enlightenment, the 'New Lights' have been read as intellectual progenitors of the United Irish movement. Dr William Drennan proudly invoked the memory of his father, Thomas Drennan, minister of First Belfast Congregation, and of his coterie, including Abernathy and Enlightenment luminary Francis Hutcheson, Professor of Moral Philosophy in the University of Glasgow.[14] More generally though the correlation is too neat. Other prominent United Irishmen, more radical than Drennan, such as Samuel Neilson – another son of the manse, and a lay elder – and McCracken, belonged to the orthodox (or 'Old Light') Third Belfast. Henry Joy's paternal grandmother, after the covenanting way, did not hold with 'set days', working the spinning wheel at her *window* on Christmas Day.[15]

The concept of 'national character' is currently unfashionable. Collective identities are more usually analysed in terms of cultural and ideological 'construction', even 'manufacture', and refuse any premise of a primordial, 'essentialist', or innate condition. When an early historian of Belfast observed that 'the bulk of the population is composed of the descendants of Scots; and it would be needless to protract a decision on their disposition and character, by waiting for relaxed or unguarded moments. They are the same at all times, and in all situations', he placed them outside history. Nonetheless it would be negligent to ignore the element of amateur ethnography that punctuates so much reportage, travel-writing, and polemic, or to dismiss it as merely impressionistic. As that inveterate purveyor of 'Englishness' George Orwell put it: national 'myths which are believed in tend to become true'.[16] It is a matter of self-image. The composite Ulsterman is supposedly direct, prudent, persevering, and economical with language, as well as with money; he is, to use his own word, 'dour'. There is no evidence that Henry Joy McCracken ever interrogated that regional stereotype, as when he pronounced Dubliners 'a set of Gasconaders, in every respect unlike Northerners'.[17]

'Belfast' noted a French traveller in the late 1790s, 'has almost entirely the look of a Scotch town, and the character of the inhabitants has considerable resemblance to that of the people of Glasgow.' Since he goes on to describe the keen local interest in goods and prices, he clearly had the industrious, enterprising, Scots stereotype in mind.[18] If those traits are attributable to a Protestant work ethic, the political personality of the Ulster Presbyterian is more demonstrably disclosed by a rhetoric of Calvinist certainty and immovable principle. The harshest insult in the locker of Covenanter invective is 'backsliding'. 'Be not unstable or wavering, carried about with every wind of doctrine' warned the *Necessary Representation* in 1649. A County Tyrone congregation in 1793 knew its 'own principles and could look with silent contempt on all calumnies and their authors'.[19] Jemmy Hope believed that 'the republican spirit, inherent in the Presbyterian community, kept resistance to arbitrary power still alive'.[20] Or perhaps it was simpler, more elemental, than that. Not all Presbyterians, after all, graduated to republicanism, and yet the first republican 'martyr', William Orr, hanged at Carrickfergus, announced from the scaffold, 'I am no traitor! I am persecuted for a persecuted country. Great Jehovah receive my soul. I die in the true faith of a Presbyterian.' Less than a year later Henry Joy McCracken sent his mother a ring from his prison cell, inscribed 'To the sacred memory of Mr. Wm. Orr, who died for his country at the altar of British Tyranny, 1797'.[21]

CHAPTER TWO

The Joys and the McCrackens

The French traveller de Latocnaye was struck by the commercial zest of late eighteenth-century Belfast and the mercantile and manufacturing cast of the town's radical cadre is correspondingly conspicuous. Samuel Neilson owned a prosperous drapery business. On a visit to Belfast in October, 1791, Wolfe Tone toured William Sinclair's large linen bleaching green, 'a noble concern [with] extensive machinery'. The first man in Ulster to use American potash in the bleaching process, Sinclair, along with Tone, had recently joined the newly founded Society of United Irishmen.[1] Henry Joy was born into this business and political world. On a slightly later trip north, Tone went to 'see McCracken's new ship, the *Hibernia*.'[2] The Belfast radicals of the time were thus more Jacobin than *sans culotte* and were exposed to the same social contradictions as their French exemplars. 'All improvement' – or labour-saving mechanization – introduced by Sinclair, notes Tone, met with popular resistance.[3] In the 1790s 'Bourgeois' champions of 'the people' were themselves resistant to the nascent trade unionism of journeymen combinations. Such tensions troubled the fierce democrat in Henry Joy McCracken, a textiles manufacturer and employer (and Ulster Scot!) who once confessed, 'I hate money, it makes me melancholy to think about it.'[4]

In addition to civic status, parliamentary representation, and local government, however oligarchic, the benefits of incorporation included trading privileges, monopolies, and immunities in a highly regulated early-modern market economy. The rise of the port of Belfast during the course of the seventeenth century was partly an economic function of the decline, as a port, of the Chichester's other town, Carrickfergus. The first earl, Arthur, rebuilt Belfast Castle, more a grand residence than a fortification, which nonetheless dominated the modest urban horizon. But as Lord Deputy of Ireland he did not typically reside there. In 1625 he took up permanent residence in the family crypt, in Saint Nicholas Church, Carrickfergus. The second earl, Arthur's brother Edward, established a firmer presence in Belfast, signifying an incremental tilt in the regional centre of political, and soon commercial, gravity. In addition to its commanding medieval castle, Carrickfergus at the time hosted the courts of assize, the county gaol, and the customs house. 'The Carrickfergus Privilege' extended to a share in the duties collected in Belfast and although this was relinquished to the crown in 1637 in exchange for a capital payment of £3000, the continued location of the customs house ten miles along the coast had administrative costs for Belfast's merchants. A 1673 merchants' petition to relocate the customs house appears to have been successful. Meanwhile in the early 1670s the number of Belfast ships arriving in Glasgow overtook the traffic from Carrickfergus. In 1685 Belfast's mapmaker Thomas Philips boasted of a harbour 'having never less than forty or fifty sail of ships always before it' and suggested that Carrickfergus castle should be demolished to provide building material for the enlargement of the burgeoning port to its south.[5]

The population of Belfast rose from around 1000 in 1650 to an estimated 5000 in 1706.[6] The port's main exports were provisions, especially butter and linen, and the merchant class invested profitably in a diversifying local economy. For example, the town acquired its first printing press in 1694. Among its earliest titles were The Bible and *The Solemn League and Covenant*; however, the sociology of the seventeenth-century merchant community, as delineated by Jean Agnew, was based on the kinship networks and business partnerships of churchmen of mainly English stock. Even George Macartney, a lowland Scot who arrived in Belfast in 1649, from Auckinleck in the covenanting heartland of Ayrshire, was conformist in religion.

Macartney's career exemplifies the business and political life of Belfast in this period. Admitted a freeman in 1652 and appointed a burgess in 1659, he served as sovereign nine times, beginning in 1662. Macartney also became County Sheriff of Antrim and a customs officer. He had interests in an iron works, a sugar refinery, and corn mills. His cousin and fellow merchant, 'Black George' Macartney, likewise served as sovereign and sheriff, while in the eighteenth century his son George, another sometime sovereign, sat for the borough of Belfast in the Irish parliament. Clearly the Macartney's enjoyed good relations with their landlords, the Earls of Donegall; and in 1719 George Jnr is recorded as 'by far' the largest tenant on the Chichester rent rolls.[7] Ironically, in the fractious political climate at the end of Queen Anne's reign, local Tory belligerents accused Presbyterian merchants of monopolising trade among themselves. Revealingly, some 80 'conformist inhabitants' of the town responded to the charge by certifying 'that the Presbyterian inhabitants of Belfast deal and trade with us as freely and readily as they with one another.'[8]

By 1714 Presbyterians were in a majority, and in the economic sphere the predominant kinship and business networks of the merchant elite began to devolve to the likes of the Joys and the McCrackens. The patriarch of the Whig-commercial Joy-McCracken connection was Francis Joy (1697–1790). There are two versions of his ancestry – descending from French Huguenot refugees named Joyeuse, or from English planters – a captain

Thomas Joy settled in County Antrim in 1612.[9] In either case, in the course of the seventeenth-century the family had assimilated to the prevailing Presbyterian dispensation. In 1720 Francis Joy, a notary and conveyancer, originally from the village of Killead in south Antrim, married Margaret Martin, granddaughter of George Martin, sovereign of Belfast in the late 1640s. They had three children, Henry (1720), Robert (1722) and Ann (1730). In 1737 Francis purchased a printing press and launched the *Belfast News-Letter*, soon established as Ireland's most successful provincial newspaper. In its combination of liberal, patriot, opinion, shipping intelligence, and business advertising, the *News-Letter* catches the political and commercial spirit of the Joy family, and of Belfast in the latter half of the eighteenth century – before, that is, the intense political polarisation of the 1790s squeezed the paper's Whig constitutionalist constituency into a 'moderate' rump.

In 1745 Francis Joy handed over control of the *News-Letter*, the print shop, and the notary's office to his sons and moved to Randalstown, where he continued on his entrepreneurial way, investing locally in a paper mill, a flax mill, and a bleaching green. Henry and Robert proved equally dynamic businessmen. Robert, in partnership with Thomas McCabe, introduced cotton manufacture to Ulster and after encountering the latest technology on a visit to Scotland, pioneered the use of textile spinning machinery in the north. The first bales of cotton were delivered to Belfast from the West Indies by Captain John McCracken, who also started up a sail cloth business and a rope works. McCracken married Ann Joy, sister of Henry and Robert. In addition to the family newspaper, Henry's paper mill in Cromac dock produced books and other goods. Cumulatively the commercial advertisements published in a single issue of the *News-Letter* at the end of 1774 present the picture of a thriving port and local economy. Recently imported goods for sale by various merchants included:

English roll tobacco and pipes, tin plates, powder and shot, lump and brown sugar, rice, French barley, coffee, chocolate, dying stuff, spades and shovels, buckles, buttons, locks, fire irons, bellows, shot bags and snuff boxes, 'with a great many more articles'.[10]

The business of business is business, but in the 'age of improvement' as the eighteenth century is often designated, 'wealth-creation' (and inheritance) carried political and social responsibilities, as well as Christian obligations. The great themes of political and economic theory, or political economy, were economic growth – improvement – and international trade. And international trade rivalries and imperial trade regulation were, consequently, intensely political issues. The *leitmotiv* of Irish patriot grievance in this period was London-imposed restrictions on Irish exports – classically on wool – whilst the legislative and practical promotion of commerce and improvement were viewed as a public good, and as nation-building endeavour (although pamphleteers and politicians referred typically to the 'Kingdom of Ireland'). Greater prosperity benefited society at large in this world view, and even radicals like Thomas Russell in the 1790s – who saw inequality, social injustice, and economic exploitation, were the conventional imagined gainful employment – stopped short of advocating wholesale wealth redistribution. Much less radical figures than Russell, however, also acknowledged that the poor are always with us, and believed that something ought to be done about that.

Captain John McCracken started the Marine Charitable Society for aged and indigent seamen. Henry Joy served as secretary to the Belfast Charitable Society, established in 1752, and Robert laid the foundation stone to Poor House in 1771 (completed in 1774).[11] The imperatives of Christian charity and of civic philanthropy fused. In 1818 Henry Joy Jnr, son of Robert, an old school Whig, and the third – and last – Joy editor and proprietor of the *News-Letter* (he sold the title in 1795), delivered a lecture entitled 'Remarks on public charity, with an account of the rise, progress, and state of charitable foundations in Belfast', which reveals the *mentalité* of his father's generation, at least as he understood it.[12] It is a profoundly Protestant vision. 'The blessings of industry are innumerable' he begins, and industry is essential to the happiness of individuals, the wellbeing of communities, and the strength of nations. Combined with liberty it sustains British imperial expansion and anchors public morals, whereas sluggish 'countries that don't enjoy the blessings of industry, are most prone to superstition'. Peru, for example. Work must be encouraged and any system of Poor Rates avoided. Dispensing 'free' relief to the needy creates dependency and idleness, thereby perpetuating the problem it is meant to fix. 'Our fathers', he concludes, 'laid the first stone of their institution on the principle of voluntary contributions; by which every annual appeal excites the best sympathies of our nature'.

The 'institution' is the Poor House, an elegant redbrick structure erected on high ground on the northern edge of the town; funded by public subscription and the sale of lottery tickets, and built on land donated by Arthur Chichester, the fifth Earl (in 1791 created First Marquess) of Donegall. Donegall also granted lands for the construction of the Exchange (1769), to which the Assembly Rooms were added (1776) and for the White Linen Hall (1783). These public buildings symbolise the civic spirit, economic growth, and demographic expansion, of late eighteenth-century Belfast, and mark a turning-point in the relationship between the town and its Donegall landlords.

When Belfast Castle was destroyed by fire in 1708, the young Fourth Earl left to join 'The list of the absentees of Ireland' and live on his mother's Staffordshire estate in England. Absentee landlords featured prominently in patriot complaint, as parasites who leached wealth from the country in the form of rents and put nothing back in in return. Economic historians may be sceptical about the actual scale and impact of these income transfers upon the Irish economy at the time, but the delinquency of the Fourth Earl of Donegall, who eventually declined into mental incapacity, is not in doubt. As Sean Connolly observes, in 1757 the Fifth Earl 'entered upon a seriously dilapidated inheritance' of legal entanglement and in Belfast and its south Antrim hinterland stunted economic development.[13] The new landlord remained an absentee in Staffordshire and in his London town house, but he did engage with Belfast, and repaired his inheritance to significant effect.

The crucial reform is what Henry Joy Jnr called the 'grand reletting of his estates' on a visit to Ireland in 1767.[14] Short-term tenures, which discouraged the improvement of properties, were commuted to 99 year leases, which regulated, in the manner of contemporary Dublin and Edinburgh, the height of new buildings and specified the quality of the materials – brick and slate – used in their construction. The streetscape walked by Volunteers and United Irishmen began to take shape. Meanwhile the workforce and general population continued to increase. By 1788 the cotton industrialist Nathaniel Wilson employed an estimated 3,000 hands.[15] Between 1780 and 1800 the number of inhabitants rose sharply from *c.* 13,000 to *c.* 20,000. That is, to be sure, roughly one tenth the size of the population of pre-union Dublin, yet for a town of such modest proportions Belfast developed a remarkably rich 'civil society' – or, as some prefer, 'public sphere'.

Institutions, organisations, and associations, included a newspaper (1737), a charitable society (1752), taverns, coffee houses, and masonic lodges, three Presbyterian congregations, the imposing, neo-classical, Saint Anne's, episcopal church (1776), and the un-steepled Saint Mary's, Catholic church (1784), the first Volunteer company (1778), a Chamber of Commerce (1783), a reading society and circulating library (1788), the Northern Whig Club (1790), the first Society of United Irishman (1791), a second newspaper, *The Northern Star* (1792), and the Belfast Society for Promoting Knowledge (1792), which evolved from the reading club and founded the Linen Hall Library (1792). All of this sociability, all of this buying and selling and giving, reading, meeting, drinking, parading, and praying happened in a distinctly Whig political culture.

The popular eighteenth-century practice of after-dinner toasting provides a sort of anthology of commonplace political sentiment. What is striking about the toasts recorded in Belfast in 1770, 1774, and 1790 is their British Whig frame of reference. Among the list of toasts communicated in 1770 by 'a numerous and respectable meeting, at the Donegall Arms', 'To the Committee for conducting the free press in Dublin' were:

> The Bill of Rights and its supporters – The Glorious and Immortal memory of King William.
> The wooden walls of England
> [The seventeenth-century Whig martyrs] Hampden – Sidney – Russell,
> [And], The American colonies, and may the descendants of those who fled from tyranny in one country, never be forced to its galling yoke in another.

Another round in 1774 included:

> Magna Carta,
> Religion without priestcraft,
> Hampden, Sidney, Russell,
> The liberty of the press and speedy repeal of the Stamp Act,
> Wisdom and firmness to the American assemblies, justice and moderation to the legislature of Britain, that their dispute may be happily settled.

And finally, at the celebration of the 1790 County Antrim general election results:

> The free states of America,
> A speedy and complete establishment of the free Gallic constitution,
> The Glorious and Immortal memory of King William,
> Hampden, Russell.[16]

In this last sample the early impact of the French Revolution is registered but overall the rhetoric of political opposition remains securely fixed in the British Whig tradition.

Protestant patriots felt no tension between their aspiration towards greater Irish constitutional autonomy, and the assertion of British Whig principle. In the 1740s, for example, the Dublin polemicist, Dr Charles Lucas, stretched his critique of constitutional subordination into condemnation of the historic misrule of the English in Ireland, and yet this prolific vindicator of Protestant nationalism occasionally signed himself 'Britannicus'. As the salutes to American liberty indicate, English-speaking protestants within the 'British Atlantic' imperial jurisdiction shared – with distinctive local variation – a political vocabulary, and a version of history, grounded in the 'Glorious Revolution' of 1688. And, as Belfast's thriving trade with the colonies shows, that imagined international community rested on a firm material foundation, for the time being anyway. After 1763, as the American crisis deepened, the 'base and superstructure' of empire began to fracture.

The American crisis, War of Independence, and Revolution disturbed the political climate across these islands, and nowhere more so than in Ulster. English reformers, often nonconformists, generally opposed crown, and government, polices of coercing the colonies, whereas the 'Moderate'-controlled Presbyterian Church of Scotland supported the London administration on America. So much for the innate democratic, even republican, ethos of Presbyterianism. The crucial difference, of course, between the Scots and their Ulster brethren, is that in Scotland by this time Presbyterians belonged to the established Church, whereas in Ireland they were still dissenters. Moreover, in addition to their Whig-patriot predisposition towards the colonist's cause – and their extensive trading relationships – Ulster's Presbyterians had many direct family connections with America.[17] Significant emigration from the north of Ireland to the colonies continued steadily throughout the eighteenth century, peaking in 1773, when, in the parlance of shipping advertisements, around 10,000 'passengers, servants, and redemptioners' embarked for the New World from Newry, Derry, and Belfast.[18] Once there, these hereditary dissenters, the 'Scotch-Irish' as they became known, took up the American cause with signature conviction.

The first page of *The Belfast News-Letter* on 3 January 1775 carried two long letters on the American crisis. One, signed under the gloriously inapt pseudonym 'MODERATUS', calls for calm on both sides, proceeds even-handedly in argument and exposition, and then ends with a classic conservative swipe at the folly of abstract thought:

> if Americans were immoderately taxed, they would have a right to complain. But that is not the case. . . . when the Americans quote a speculative writer, such as Mr Locke, they shew their want of judgement and give up their cause. Are the closet reveries of an author to direct the operations of government to over-rule the parliament and to destroy the constitution?

The other, signed by yet another 'BRITANNICUS', concludes, 'no proposition can be more self-evident than that the trade of the Mother Country with the colonies can never be secured unless the latter are governed by the laws of the Mother Country'.[19] By the standards of the partisan times this amounts to fair coverage, although that is not how a critic in the *Dublin Mercury* read it:

> The Puritan Journal impressed in Belfast,
> Exhibits the printer's complexion and cast,
> Whose partial accounts of each public transaction,
> Proclaim him the infamous tool of a faction.
> . . . . .
> the low scribe of a party quite fanatic,
> With zeal for their Brethren across the Atlantic,
> Discreetly and piously chuses to tell
> No tidings but such as come posting from Hell.[20]

The American war that began the following year aroused political sympathy in Ulster, and severely disrupted the Irish economy, especially the textiles industry, as trading to the colonies came to an abrupt halt. Then in 1778 France entered the war on the American side, exposing the island of Ireland to potential attack, even invasion. Its manpower, military, and fiscal resources stretched to their limits, the British government could not hope to adequately maintain its garrison in Ireland. On the very day, 17 March, that Britain declared war on France, Robert Joy convened a meeting in his Belfast home to form a company of volunteers to defend the island against the French threat.[21] It was a momentous initiative. Popular militias – the armed citizen – as guarantor of liberty, as opposed to standing armies that endangered it, is a core value of classical republican theory, and 'real Whig' ideology – although Henry Grattan's description of the movement which rapidly emerged as 'the armed property of the nation' more nearly catches its orientation. In either case, the Volunteers soon turned their attention to politics.

In the 1790s Wolfe Tone claimed disingenuously that upon 'closer examination into the situation of my native country', he made 'a grand discovery, tho' I might have found it in Swift or Molyneux, that the influence of England was the radical vice of our government, and consequently that Ireland would never be either free, prosperous, or happy, until she was independent'.[22] William Molyneux's *Case of Ireland being bound by acts of parliament in England, stated* (1698), an extended legal and historical vindication of constitutional autonomy, was perhaps best remembered for the occasion of its publication, a Westminster-imposed prohibition on the export of wool. Jonathan Swift's *A Proposal for the Universal Use of Irish Manufactures* (1720) called for the burning of 'everything English but their coals', and indeed in the late 1770s Dublin protestors led by James Napper Tandy responded to the economic downturn caused by the American war by organising (sometimes by intimidating shopkeepers) 'non-importation agreements' on English goods.

Outside east Ulster, where it originated, Volunteering put most boots on the ground in Dublin – together the two most politically literate areas in Ireland, the two hardest hit, especially in the textiles trades, by wartime economic dislocation, and the two sites of an unprecedented mass political mobilisation.[23] On 4 November, 1779, the birthday of William III, the Volunteers, Horse and Foot, rallied at his equestrian statue facing the parliament in College Green; a placard hung from the barrel of a cannon demanded 'Free Trade, or Else'. Indoors a group of reinvigorated Patriot MPs led loosely by Grattan, pressed for the repeal of commercial restrictions. Later that month Lord North's ministry in London, confronted, at a moment of imperial overextension, by the prospect of unrest in Ireland, lifted constraints on Irish trade.

'Free Trade' was a signal victory for the Volunteer-Patriot axis, and in retrospect it appears as a major instalment in a sequence of reforms: a modest Catholic Relief Act (1778), the repeal of the Test and Corporation acts (1780), and the amendment of 'Poynings' Law' and the repeal of the Declaratory Act (1782). The Test and Corporation acts excluded Protestant dissenters from local government office, and in 1781 Henry Joy snr, town clerk between 1759 and 1772, became the first Belfast Presbyterian Burgess since 1707.[24] Preceded by the celebrated Dungannon Volunteer convention, the so-called 'Constitution of 1782' devolved the right to initiate legislation to the commons, and restored appellate jurisdiction to the lords. Patriots leaders, such as Grattan, and his sponsor, and Volunteer Commander-in- Chief, the Earl of Charlemont, were more or less satisfied with this outcome; others, such as Henry Flood in parliament, and the likes of Tandy, and future United Irish ideologue, Dr William Drennan, were not.

The lethal flaw (from a Patriot point of view) in the 'Constitution of 1782' was that London retained control of the Irish executive – 'Dublin Castle' – and thus, through the distribution of patronage, of parliament. To counteract the exercise of such irresponsible power the politically advanced now pushed on for franchise reform. The Volunteer movement split, and in November 1783, when Flood, in Volunteer uniform, marched onto the floor of the House of Commons, to present the petition of the Dublin reform convention, he was accused of attempting to intimidate the legislature. If so, he failed. Also in 1783 the admission of Catholics to some companies in Dublin and Belfast ignored the penal law forbidding papists from carrying arms, and further divided the unified movement of 1782.

Volunteering ran out of steam in the second half of the decade; although it proved a seminal experience for Belfast reformers nonetheless, and played a crucial role in the radical revival of the early 1790s. Henry Joy McCracken was too young to join the First Belfast Company in 1778, although his two older brothers, Frank and William, and his cousin Henry Joy Jnr, did enrol. McCracken was a true son of the Belfast of his time, and of the Presbyterian, civic-minded, Joy-McCracken extended family. In 1788, with his sister Mary Ann, he opened a short-lived non-denominational Sunday School.[25] He also belonged, in a sort of second order way, to a business dynasty. Writing to Mary Ann from Dublin, in May 1798, he describes the mood on the streets of a city on the eve of rebellion – 'the people expect to have the soldiers living at free quarters' – but not before reporting on the poor seller's market for 'fancy goods' and for their 'mother's cambrics'.[26] Town and family undoubtedly shaped, but did not *determine*, Henry Joy McCracken's politics. He made choices, and chose to go further than, for example, his older kinsman, the Whig-Patriot Volunteer, Henry Joy Jnr, who tried to stall the town's embrace of the Catholic cause in 1791–2, who carried a travel pass during the rebellion (signed by Castlereagh, nemesis of the Belfast United Irishmen), and whose voluminous papers on the histories of Belfast and his family are silent on the life and fate of his McCracken cousin. [27]

CHAPTER THREE

Citizen

Henry Joy McCracken was born on 31 August 1767 in 39 High Street, Belfast, fourth of the six children of Captain John McCracken and Ann Joy. His siblings were Margaret (1760), Francis (1762), William (1765), Mary Ann (1770), and John (1772). Although a well-disposed writer tells us that he was 'a very apple blossom of a baby', little is actually known about Henry Joy's childhood, indeed even during his political career in the 1790s he sometimes drops out of the historical record.[1] Unlike his comrades Thomas Russell and Theobald Wolfe Tone, he did not keep diaries, or journals, or write pamphlets. Almost all of the correspondence that does survive are letters written from prison in 1796 to 1797 – and on occasion his sister, Mary Ann, complained about their brevity.[2] A talented mimic in his youth; later in the convivial, hard-drinking world of clandestine politics he had a reputation for being able to hold his tongue.[3] Most of the evidence concerning his personality, character, and beliefs, comes from very partisan sources, Mary Ann, who adored him, and Jemmy Hope, who by his own testimony admired McCracken above all others.[4] Of course, the plain fact that 'Harry' commanded such loyalty tells its own tale.

Scripture formed the bedrock of Henry Joy's early education. A protestant dissenter, he and his family belonged, as did Samuel Neilson, to the 'Old Light' Third Belfast Presbyterian congregation, and in later years he forged a political and personal friendship with that Church's minister, the Revd Sinclair Kelburn, literally a 'Christian Soldier' famous locally for preaching in his Volunteer uniform. Young Harry, as his family called him, attended the school of David Manson, a gifted teacher whose methods would today be described as 'progressive'– sparing the rod to nurture the child. In addition, his father who had been captured by the French during the Seven Years' War and briefly held prisoner hired an old French weaver in town to teach his children the language.[5] Years later Mary Ann urged Harry when he was in gaol not to forget his 'French dictionary, syntax, and grammar, all which are very necessary at present as almost everybody in Belfast are learning French'.[6]

Early on Henry Joy also displayed an aptitude for 'mechanics', and that together with his lack of literary production suggests a particular cast of mind. Wolfe Tone portrayed himself as 'a very plain man', who disliked 'abstract reasoning on practical subjects', and 'wasting time in proving' axioms.[7] In fact that rhetorical construction more accurately fits his friend McCracken. In 1791 when some northern dissenters balked at the prospect of supporting the campaign for Catholic relief, Tone won many of them over by publishing a closely reasoned, fluently written pamphlet, *An Argument of Behalf of the Catholics of Ireland*. But Catholics were thin on the ground in Belfast. In contrast to the sectarian demographics confronting their country cousins in east Tyrone and north Armagh to Belfast Presbyterians Catholics were a largely unknown, only notionally threatening, quantity. So, wasting no time on theoretical axioms, Henry Joy assuaged any lingering ancestral anxieties the McCracken clan might have had about the perils of popery by pointing to the one Catholic whom they *knew* well, the family's trusted servant Betty.[8]

Tone started out as a barrister, Russell joined the British Army, and McCracken went into the textiles business, working for the family firm, first at the loom, then in the 'counting house'. In 1789 he travelled to Scotland – the first and only time he left Ireland – to recruit skilled calico printers and mechanics; he also acted as salesman for his mother and sister's muslin goods, and in that year was promoted to manager of the mill.[9] Apprenticed in 1785, aged 18, he had entered the workplace at a time when the Volunteer movement was winding down, and who then could have foreseen the epochal political turmoil of the coming decade? McCracken and his cohort made political choices that changed the course – and abruptly shortened the duration – of their lives, but they did so in circumstances not of their making. If the French Revolution had not happened, who today would have heard of the provincial merchant, the jobbing lawyer, and a junior officer on half pay?

The French Revolution was a world-historical event. In William Wordsworth's famous lines:

> Bliss it was in that dawn to be alive
> But to be young was very heaven.

And remaking the world is generally the pursuit of the young. In 1789 Wordsworth turned 19; Tone, Lord Edward Fitzgerald, and Arthur O'Connor were 26, Thomas Addis Emmet and Jemmy Hope were 25, and Russell and McCracken 22. Conversely, older radicals such as Dr William Drennan, and the Catholic Committee leader and United Irishman John Keogh, aged respectively 35 and 49 in 1789, retired from the field as the politics of reform turned to the preparation of insurrection. Drennan's exact contemporary, the hereditary Whig Henry Joy Jnr, saw out the revolutionary decade in the service of the state as a Yeoman, with Lord Castlereagh's travel pass in his back-pocket. None of this is to posit an iron law of history: the veteran radical Napper Tandy, 52 years old in 1789, stayed the course, whereas the 20-year-old Castlereagh, victorious popular candidate for County Down in the 1790 general election, turned counter-revolutionary apostate. But the pattern is firm enough to bear generalisation. Bliss was it in that dawn for the young Henry Joy McCracken to be alive.

The full impact on Ireland of the unfolding events in France were not instantaneous. In retrospect the vigour and success of the electoral campaigns in June 1790, in the 'open' constituencies of Dublin, Antrim, and Down, portended popular political revival after the lull of the late 1780s, and the procession in Belfast celebrating victory in County Antrim featured the figure of HIBERNIA, holding aloft the cap of liberty.[10] However, there is no recorded celebration there of Bastille Day on the 14 July 1790. The actual catalyst for resurgent political mobilisation appears to have been the public debate ignited by Edmund Burke's *Reflections on the Revolution in France*, published in November 1790, and Thomas Paine's demotic, democratic riposte *Rights of Man*, published in March 1791. Written in a readily accessible style Paine's blistering polemic against monarchy, aristocracy, and the hereditary principle reached large audiences across the Atlantic world, and particularly so in Ireland. Tone called it 'the Koran of Blefuscu'.[11]

By the spring of 1791 the dissemination of Paineite ideas and the inspiration of the French example (some antagonists of the revolution said the French disease) helped to re-energise volunteering and the politics of parliamentary reform. Reformers sought to make the legislature more representative, and responsible to 'the people', by extending the franchise (eventually advocating universal manhood suffrage), eliminating voting based on narrow property qualifications, or arcane chartered privilege (which the Belfast Corporation borough exemplified), and disbarring from subsequent office MPs in receipt of government sinecures or pensions. They thus spoke the language of Christopher Wyvill, The Yorkshire Association, and other English reformers, since at least the 1770s. But in Ireland, as became apparent in the political agitations of

1783 of 1784, the reform agenda had first to come to terms with the Catholic Question.

Despite their bishops and most of the clergy, Irish Catholics were as receptive to French stimuli as their protestant neighbours. Indeed, in one crucial way events in France advanced the case for Catholic relief from the penal laws. According to their political opponents Catholics, raised in a culture of institutional hierarchy, unquestioning obedience, and inbred subservience, were unfit for liberty. Yet now the most powerful, most populous, and *Catholic,* nation in Europe had thrown off the yoke of tyranny. New Catholic leaders, notably the Dublin textiles merchants, John Keogh and Richard McCormick, soon showed their contempt for the traditional deference towards authority displayed by the remnants of Catholic aristocracy and their episcopal allies (in 1792 Keogh referred acidly to certain bishops as 'old men, used to bend to power').[12] The elements in a seminal realignment of Irish politics began to slot into place – and in a real sense the author of that 'new departure' was a then little-known Dublin barrister, Theobald Wolfe Tone.

In July 1790 Tone, a fledgling Whig pamphleteer, and Thomas Russell chanced to meet in the public gallery of the Irish House of Commons and quickly became fast friends. Together they set up a political club, or private debating society, whose members included Thomas Addis Emmet and Drennan. Then in September Russell moved north to take up a commission in the 64th regiment where he mixed freely in the well-lubricated sociable milieu of radical Belfast. It was Russell who invited Tone to draft the resolutions to be adopted by the Volunteers and inhabitants of Belfast at the celebration of Bastille Day, 14 July 1791. The resolutions identified English influence as the source of Ireland's ills, and parliamentary reform as the remedy. This is standard stuff, but Tone went further. No reform, he stated, would be 'just or efficacious' which did not include the Catholics. For some in the gathering that day he had gone too far, too soon, and the third resolution was rejected. The disappointed author of the resolutions now turned his pen to a pamphlet, addressed primarily to dissenters haunted by the spectre of popery.

In *An Argument on Behalf of the Catholics of Ireland* Tone appealed to the historical record, principle – the universal rights of man – and recent French and American experience, to acquit his penalised fellow countrymen of the charges of priestcraft, super-stition, and Jacobitism, of owing allegiance to the Pope in temporal affairs, and of nursing ambitions to overturn the seventeenth-century land settlements. But his main argument is instrumental, urging his readers to 'look to their fellow slaves, who by coalition with them may rise to be their fellow citizens and form a new order in their society, a new era in their history. Let them once cry *Reform and the Catholics*, and Ireland is free, independent and happy.'[13] Republished in up to five editions over the next six months the *Argument* sold in the tens of thousands, and is a foundational document of the Society of United Irishmen, formed in Belfast in mid-October, 1791.

Curiously, Henry Joy McCracken is not listed as a member of the original United Society, and yet the omnivorous antiquarian, Francis J. Bigger, refers to the papers of Samuel Neilson in his possession as dating 'from the period of his founding of the Society of United Irishmen, in conjunction with Thomas Russell and Henry McCracken, and with the subsequent cooperation of T. W. Tone.'[14] Excepting Russell and Tone, the members of the original Society were drawn from the ranks of the First Belfast Volunteer company, those who were more democratic in their politics and more sanguine on Catholic rights than the Northern Whig Club old guard: town worthies like Waddell Cunningham, Dr Alexander Haliday (both slave-owning proprietors of West

Indian sugar plantations), the Revd William Bruce, and Henry Joy
Jnr, who all shared Lord Charlemont's 'gradualist' approach to
Catholic relief.[15]

The Belfast Society was small, bourgeois and, again excepting
Russell and Tone, Presbyterian. The Dublin Society founded a
few weeks later in November 1791 was larger – over 400 in number
over its three-year life span – and also mostly middle class with a
personnel composed of Catholic and Protestant in roughly equal
proportions.[16] Indeed there was a considerable overlap at this early
stage in the membership of the Dublin United Irishmen and the
Catholic Committee, signalling a radicalising of Catholic politics.
When the Catholic Society of Dublin's Declaration broke the
convention of petitioning for partial relief by calling for the repeal
of all penal laws, it was repudiated, at the behest of Dublin Castle,
by the Catholic titular peer, Lord Kenmare. However, the days of
deferring to aristocrats, and to government, were apparently at an
end. In the first concerted mobilisation of expressly Catholic
public opinion, Kenmare was denounced at county meetings, and
ridiculed in the press, as 'Lord Lickspittle, the Kerry traitor.'[17]
Mocked and brought to heel, Kenmare, and his associates Lord
Fingal and the archbishop of Dublin, Thomas Troy, grudgingly
fell into line with the Catholic Committee's more assertive tactics.

The Kenmare episode confirmed the political leadership of the
merchant and manufacturing elite within Catholic politics, which
in turn presented the British government with a problem. London
now attempted to detach the Catholics from their developing
alignment with the northern dissenters – in effect to counteract
Tone's strategy – by offering a new instalment of relief. Even the
Protestant ultras in the pensioned and patronaged Dublin parliament had no option but to vote through 'the king's business' as
communicated from Whitehall. However, the 1792 Relief Act did
not placate the Catholics as intended. First, it was too limited,

allowing Catholics to practice law for example, but stopping short of the franchise; and second, and at least as importantly, the compensatory carnival of anti-popish rhetoric that passed for debate in the House of Commons enraged the people the legislation was supposed to conciliate. The class register of the unparliamentary invective is striking. Keogh and his cohort were taunted as 'shopkeepers' and *therefore* as unrepresentative of the wider Catholic community. The Catholic Committee soon demonstrated otherwise.

1792 turned into a year of intense political drama. In January the United Irishmen in Belfast launched a newspaper, the *Northern Star* edited by Neilson, and efficiently distributed throughout Ulster and beyond. The Catholic Committee organised nationwide county elections of delegates to attend a convention in Dublin in December and put their popular mandate beyond question. Wolfe Tone replaced Edmund Burke's son Richard as agent to the Committee. Meanwhile in the countryside, in the borderlands of Ulster and Leinster the mounting violence of the Defenders – a lower class Catholic secret society – caused growing apprehension and bewilderment among local magistrates and in governing circles alike. Supporters of the establishment in Church and State met these several challenges by proclaiming the doctrine of 'Protestant ascendancy' – a Protestant parliament and state apparatus for a Protestant people – first by Dublin Corporation, then by sixteen county grand juries. The counter-mobilisation of loyalist opinion could not, however, prevent the convention, which duly met in the capital on 2 December, 1792.

The convention, known colloquially as the Back Lane parliament, adopted a motion to petition for a repeal of all penal laws, proposed by a close associate of Neilson, the Lisburn linen merchant Luke Teeling, and decided to bypass the Castle and present the petition directly to the King. Tone accompanied the delegation to London. The British government continued its policy of conciliating the

Catholics as a way of decoupling them from the *de facto* alliance with the radicals, symbolised by the presence of Mr Tone in London, and at a moment when the northerners were preparing for their own Ulster convention for parliamentary reform, as in 1782, in Dungannon. The 1793 Act granted the franchise to 40-shilling free holders in county constituencies, a major concession that nevertheless fell short of the convention's demand. Catholics were still prohibited from sitting in parliament. In the event, the Catholic Committee compromised and barely acknowledged the support of the northern dissenters in their campaign. London's strategy appeared to have worked. 'As for merchants', lamented Tone, 'I begin to see they are no great hand at revolutions.'[18]

The British government hoped that the amelioration of Catholic grievance would defuse domestic disaffection in the event of war with revolutionary France, but by the Spring of 1793 its 'conciliation account' had closed.[19] The Irish government had already gone on the offensive, proscribing the Volunteers, prosecuting prominent United Irishmen, including the proprietors of the *Northern Star*, for sedition, enacting legislation restricting the import of gunpowder, prohibiting conventions, and establishing a militia. The county-based militia regiments were raised by conscription by ballot and the anti-militia riots that followed crossed new thresholds of collective violence in eighteenth-century Ireland.[20] It is characteristic of Henry Joy McCracken, a man of action, that he re-enters the historical record at this moment of escalating conflict.

On 9 March soldiers ran amok on the streets of 'the much defamed town' of Belfast, but this was more than a routine eighteenth-century fracas between the garrison and the citizenry. By one account the red coats were instructed by an officer 'not to spare leg, arm, or life', and were directed by an agent of Lord Hillsborough who 'pointed out the fit places to attack'. Certainly, the political intent of the military riot is clear, as tavern signs of the

French General, Dumouriez, Mirabeau, and Benjamin Franklin, were torn down. The following day a young man was slashed with a sword.[21] Just over a month later the second of three clashes occurred. Franklin was torn down again, and another sign from above the office of the *Northern Star*. Two drunken soldiers who had assaulted townspeople were beaten by a crowd of young men armed with sticks and 'some good weapon[s]'. As the senior officer on the scene Colonel Barber reached for his sword, Henry Joy McCracken – standing at almost 6 foot and by contemporary standards a strikingly tall figure – stepped forward, put his hand on Barber's arm and suggested he desist. The officer turning, accused him of being 'a ringleader of the mob and a rascal', to which McCracken replied that he was his equal and demanded satisfaction. Backing off, Barber declared that the place was improper, and that he didn't know his challenger. Mr Bristow, the town sovereign, would give him his name McCracken told him, and he would meet anywhere. The next morning Bristow asked Henry Joy to apologise to Barber. He refused.[22]

This street vignette is quite revealing. McCracken's fearlessness is clear, as is his sure sense of self ('I am your equal') and honour (demanding 'satisfaction' when insulted). The code of honour, and its ultimate expression, duelling, were integral to the gentlemanly culture of the time, regardless of political affiliation. The attorney general John Fitzgibbon (later Lord Chancellor, Lord Clare) declined a challenge from Napper Tandy on the grounds that he was not a gentleman, yet Tone later grudgingly conceded that while Fitzgibbon gave no quarter, he expected none.[23] Finally, McCracken's encounter with Barber exemplifies the intimate, face-to-face, world in which both men lived – 'go fetch the town sovereign, he'll tell you who I am'. Barber learned who he was soon enough and their paths would cross again in even more fateful circumstances.

George Benn describes the offending signage as 'obnoxious', and since France had declared war on Britain (and thus by extension, Ireland) on 1 February 1793, a public salute to an enemy combatant, General Dumouriez, could reasonably be read as treason.[24] It is this war that accounts for what, on 1 April, Drennan's sister, Martha McTier, called 'the sudden reverse in the complexion of the times'[25] A Colonel French, present at the meeting between McCracken, Barber, and Bristow complained about his soldiers being goaded in the streets and 'swore by God if there was one gun fired from any window at any of his people he would immediately burn the town'.[26] Open campaigning for parliamentary reform and further Catholic relief effectively came to an end. The *Northern Star* continued to publish, and the Dublin Society continued to meet although the numbers attending fell off sharply. The wartime clamp-down on radical activity should be viewed in a 'four nations' perspective. In August the leading Scottish reformer, Thomas Muir, was sentenced to 14 years transportation for sedition. In May 1794 government shut down the Dublin Society, driving it 'underground', followed the next month by the suspension of *Habeas Corpus* in Britain. Desperate times called for desperate measures. Or so the story goes.

CHAPTER FOUR

Revolutionary

It can be argued that the suspension of civil liberties and other repressive measures actually encouraged disaffection and were therefore counterproductive. It can also be argued that government assessments of radical intent were well grounded, and that certain United Irishmen were set on the road to revolution irrespective of government policy, both propositions are true. For example, the suppression of the Dublin Society seems to have been triggered by the arrest of the Revd William Jackson on a mission to Ireland to estimate the prospective levels of support for a French invasion. Jackson poisoned himself in the dock, and among his papers was a seditious memorandum drawn up for him by Wolfe Tone. Nor was this the first incriminating document in Tone's hand to come the government's way. In a letter enclosing his 1791 Belfast Bastille Day resolutions Tone confides to Russell that he had 'not said one word that looks like a wish for *separation*, tho' I give it to you & to your friends as my most decided opinion that such an event would be a *regeneration* for this country.' Two years later, almost to the day, Fitzgibbon declared in the House of Lords 'that a separation from England is the object of our agitators did not require this paper to convince us . . . they only watch for events to rebel against the Crown of Great Britain'.[1]

The evidence against Tone and Archibald Hamilton Rowan, whom Jackson had visited in prison, was circumstantial, and

Map by Ruadhán MacEoin, 2019

rather than risk a failed prosecution – and in another example of how political antagonists lived at close quarters in the 1790s – the authorities offered Tone a deal, conveyed by his old college friend, Marcus Beresford, son of John, first Commissioner of the Revenue. In return for information, not least on Rowan, Tone would be permitted to leave the country, never to return. His high sense of honour prevented him, of course, from implicating Rowan – who subsequently escaped to France – but he did supply information implicating himself. His days in Ireland were now numbered. If the Jackson affair revealed Tone's militant republican politics, these were in advance of and were shaped earlier than the views of most of his United Irish colleagues. On the other hand he was less socially radical than his closest friends and associates within the movement, such as Neilson, Russell, and McCracken.

Meanwhile as Dublin Castle closed in on Tone in the late spring of 1794, Neilson, the principal architect of United Irish strategy, set to work first in the north then in Dublin and beyond on building a secret revolutionary organisation.[2] The chronology is significant because in retrospect contemporaries and later historians identified the recall of Earl Fitzwilliam as Lord Lieutenant in February 1795, as the moment when the countdown to rebellion began. However preparations were already underway. As Fitzgibbon might have put it, the project of an independent Irish republic did not require the Fitzwilliam episode to activate it; the 'agitators' got started on their own.

Fitzwilliam was appointed Lord Lieutenant of Ireland in July 1794, as a result of the high political transactions entailed in the formation a wartime 'national' coalition government between Prime Minister William Pitt's Tories and the Whig faction led by the Duke of Portland, in which Fitzwilliam was a leading figure. His tenure in Dublin Castle proved brief – he landed in Ireland on 4 January and departed on 25 March 1795 – and consequential. In short, the new Lord Lieutenant revived the Catholic Question, allied with Irish opposition Whigs, prominently Henry Grattan and George Ponsonby, and sacked equally prominent ascendancy politicians, such as John Beresford. These dramatic interventions provoked a political backlash in official London, and aroused great expectations among Irish Catholics and reformers. Fitzwilliam had gone too far, however, especially in his treatment of Beresford, and he was abruptly recalled. This crisis stands out so vividly in accounts of the 1790s because the crash-landing of new hope for real change led many to conclude that purely political tactics and remonstrance were futile. Reform did not work. Plainly, in this analysis, revolution now amounted to nothing less than the recognition of necessity.

In the increasingly hostile political climate of post-Fitzwilliam Ireland Tone concluded it was time to go. Might he not be prosecuted after all? Taking leave of his friends in Dublin in May, he travelled with his family to Belfast, as it turned out for the final time. 'I remember particularly', he later recalled,

> two days that we passed on Cave Hill; on the first, Russell, Neilson, Simms, McCracken, and one or two more of us on the summit of MacArt's fort . . . took a solemn obligation . . . never to desist in our efforts until we have subverted the authority of England over our country and asserted our independence; another day we had the tent of the first [Belfast Volunteer] regiment pitched in the Deer Park, and a company of thirty of us, including the family of the Simms, Neilson's, McCracken's, and my own, dined and spent the day deliciously together.[3]

On 13 June 1795 Tone set sail for America aboard a ship aptly named after the famous Roman republican, *Cincinnatus*.

Henry Joy's efforts were by then well under way. In March he enrolled in the revamped, oath-bound and underground United

Irishmen, in June he joined a masonic lodge, and at some point that summer secured a deputy command in the County Antrim Defenders.[4] He thus stood at the intersection of the revolutionary forces challenging Protestant ascendancy and the British connection. McCracken, Neilson and other organisers were in effect channelling and weaponising the popular politicisation (or in conservative parlance, disaffection) that they had done so much to develop earlier in the decade. The first phase of politicisation, between 1791 and 1793 – the revival of Volunteering, the mass mobilisations of the Catholic campaigns, the renewed agitation for parliamentary reform, the spread of Defenderism – was animated by 'French principles' and democratic ideas, disseminated in the *Northern Star*, propagated by Paine's *Rights of Man*, and circulated in pamphlets, handbills, leaflets, ballads, and catechisms.

For instance, whereas Tone condemned the game laws, a totem of aristocratic privilege, resting on legal definitions of property, and routinely contested in practice by the exercise of customary right, Russell later came close to an antinomian critique of all law as a ruling class instrument of criminalisation, and a subversion of natural justice.[5] Certainly though, Tone's strictures would not have appeared even remotely more moderate than Russell's to 'Squire Firebrand', one of the eponymous characters in the Presbyterian minister James Porter's satire, *Billy Bluff and the Squire* (1796). In that pamphlet a collection of letters originally published in the *Northern Star*, the squire laments the bygoneness of his father's day, when tradesmen were horsewhipped for presenting bills and a farmer's son left to die in prison 'for shooting a partridge'.[6] In his father's time indeed, an advertisement in the *Belfast News-Letter* offered a reward of ten guineas for information leading to the 'prosecution of any person or persons who shall be seen on any part of *Lord Antrim's mountains*, with guns, dogs or nets (according to the late act of parliament).'[7]

Besides, the squire is only lightly parodied. In his journals Russell relates an episode in which an ascendancy MP threw 'a glass at a blind fid[d]ler's head' for playing a traditional Jacobite air, 'The White Cockade',[8] and from the perspective of the ruling elite, his aggression made sense. As the Scottish republican Andrew Fletcher observed almost a century before, 'if a man were permitted to make all the ballads he need not care who should make the laws of a nation.'[9] *Paddy's Resource*, a slim pocket-sized book of patriotic song first published in 1795 and updated and reprinted over the coming years – 'William Orr, an Elegy', makes it into the 1798 volume – provides a compact anthology of contemporary radical ideology. The songs counterpose liberty, virtue, reason, union, the French 'decree', and 'the Sovereign People', to tyranny, monarchy, aristocracy, and the church by law established. One, 'The Rights of Man', is set to the tune of 'God save the King', and another, 'The divine right of the Majesty of the People', ridicules crowns as 'gaudy toy[s]'.[10] But perhaps a distinction might usefully be made between 'radical' ideology, and 'popular' *mentalité*. The ballads in *Paddy's Resource* are sprinkled with sprigs of shamrock, 'Paddies', harps, and a few words and phrases in Irish – sometimes striking a note of outright condescension.

> May liberty triumph abroad and at home,
> And Paddy, when tipsy in safety get home.[11]

The original society of United Irishmen adopted the harp as it emblem, and soon enough replaced its crown with the cap of liberty. The harp, also embossed on green flags at the time, signifies the cultural nationalist dimension of fledgling Irish republicanism. In terms of intellectual history, the period of late 'enlightenment' coincides and intersects with the early development of 'romanticism'. In the second half of the eighteenth century, figures such as the leading Catholic spokesman, Charles O'Conor, and the Eton-educated, retired English general, Charles Vallancey, pioneered scholarly investigations of ancient Gaelic civilisation, and the collection of Irish antiquities. In 1789 Charlotte Brooke published *Reliques of Irish Poetry*, including translations (or as she modestly insists, paraphrase) of songs by the blind harper, Carolan. The United Irishmen, and the McCracken family, were closely involved in a seminal event in this cultural revival, the Belfast Harper's festival of 1792, organised by Edward Bunting.

A native of Armagh and orphaned young, in 1784 the 11-year-old Bunting was apprenticed to the organist in St Anne's Church, Belfast, and taken into the McCracken home, where he lived for decades to come. On 11 to 14 July 1792, he assisted Henry Joy Jnr and Dr James McDonnell, the McCracken family doctor, in arranging a harpers festival and competition. A classically trained musician, Bunting's encounter with the harpists and their traditional repertoire changed the course of his life as he began to tour the country, transcribing and collecting 'folk' songs, airs, and tunes. In 1797 he published the first of three volumes, entitled *A General Collection of the Ancient Irish music*.[12] Although a friend of Thomas Russell and an adoptive brother of Henry Joy McCracken, there is no evidence of any political engagement by Bunting; but in Belfast in the 1790s politics could scarcely be avoided. The festival coincided with the Volunteer celebration of the fall of the Bastille and the public debate about supporting Catholic relief. Wolfe Tone was in town and attended the festival. His verdict, 'strum, strum, and be hanged!' has been read as protestant anglophone indifference to native Irish culture. A closer reading confirms that the poor man had a hangover.[13]

The distribution of political information in itself subverted authority. 'The poor were not to concern themselves in what related to the government' wrote Russell. Such matters of state were to be left 'to wiser heads and to people who understand' them.[14] In contrast to that governing doctrine of priestly mystification, United Irish counter-pedagogy for the common man spoke the language of reason, science, political progress, social justice, and enlightenment. But, perhaps inevitably, some of that Paineite rationality got rubbed off in demotic translation. A catechistic leaflet in 1794 asked:

> Q. What are the common curses of mankind?
> A. The habit of affixing great ideas to little things - hence the phrase, as great as a king (although a German bastard) the first of which God gave to the Israelites, as a curse to them and their posterity – this is the divinity of kings. See Samuel, chap viii.
> Q. When will happiness attend all mankind?
> A. At the expiration of slavery, priestcraft, kingcraft, and aristocracy – thence spring fair Liberty and Equality, that man may enjoy the Blessings of God in an earthly paradise.[15]

The combination of scriptural reference, millenarianism and standard radical rhetoric is disjointed, potent, and clearly of Presbyterian provenance; it also resembles the catechistic form and subversive content of contemporaneous (Catholic) Defender documents.

Defenderism blended traditional agrarian grievances – concerning rents, tithes, and taxes – with anti-Protestantism, of the kind expressed in Irish language verse of the time and a Jacobite-style embrace of the French Revolution: the republic across the water succeeds the pretender in Ireland's imagined deliverance. Thus:

> Where did you get your commands from? First from Orleans castle we first got our commands to plant the Tree of Liberty in the Irish lands.

> The French Defenders will uphold the cause and Irish Defenders will
> pull down the British Laws.[16]

However, whilst the United Irish broadside anticipated the extirpation of priestcraft, a Defender pledge, 'to quell all nations, dethrone all kings and plant the true religion, that was lost since reformation', exposes the sectarian tensions at the core of the mass revolutionary movement that Henry Joy and other 'emissaries' began to construct in 1795.

Defender documents are peppered with gibberish words such as 'Eifitic Moctic', or 'Eliphismatis', which invoke the fabricated mysteries, and mimic the 'cabbalistic jargon' of freemasonry. Defenders likewise adopted the masonic terminology of 'brother' and 'lodge'; their County Down commander, John Magennis was even styled 'Grand Master'.[17] In theory, and sometimes in practice, Freemasons subscribed to fraternity and to a non-partisan deity, which offered an 'Enlightened' antidote to sectarian rancour. Freemasons, particularly in County Tyrone, prominently supported the campaign for parliamentary reform in 1793. McCracken and his associates, however, joined up for practical, not ideological, purposes. United Irish emissaries, proselytising and recruiting in rural Ulster and beyond, often travelled along 'trade routes' posing as textiles merchants; masonic signs and passwords granted some of them access to yet another readymade and extensive network of contacts. Stationed in mid-Ulster in 1798, General Knox testified to the range of that network when he observed that 'much treason is kept alive thro' every county in the north thro' the medium of Free Mason Lodges'.[18]

However not all masons were radicals. The Orange Order, a popular loyalist, Protestant supremacist, 'vulgar conservative' movement founded in September 1795 in north Armagh (near the border with Tyrone) drew freely on the masonic model. Popular politicisation was thus not only republican in orientation. The 1790s in fact is the decade not only of failed revolution but of successful counter-revolution; of militant mass loyalist mobilisation in defence of Protestant ascendency, social hierarchy and the British connection; of state repression descending into a systematic campaign of state terror. In the words of Thomas Paine, quoted by Henry Joy McCracken in one of his last letters, these were 'Times that try men's souls'.[19]

CHAPTER FIVE

State Prisoner

The Belfast-led transformation of the United Irishmen into a revolutionary underground organisation hinged on the co-option of an already existing mass, oath-bound movement – the Defenders. In the language of the time to be 'Up' signified membership of the United Irishmen and those who belonged to both the United Irishmen and the Defenders were 'Up and Up'. Samuel Neilson devised the underground strategy and Henry Joy McCracken, probably more than any other leadership figure, forged the alliance with the Defenders. He quickly earned the trust of 'the men of no property', with whom he had an instinctive rapport, and worked closely with Defender principals such as Charles Hamilton Teeling and the Lurgan-based textiles merchant Bernard Coyle (or Coile). Teeling, in 1795 a mere 17 years of age, played a pivotal role in making the alliance. His father Luke, a prosperous businessman who owned a bleaching green near Lisburn was, as noted earlier, an ally of Neilson's and an outspoken delegate on the floor of the Catholic Convention in 1792. Suggestively, in June 1796 Neilson joined Lisburn Masonic Lodge 193, whose other brethren included Charles's older brother, Bartholomew, and Henry Munro – both destined to hang in 1798.[1] Charles Teeling's importance within the maturing conspiracy is indicated by the fact that a day before departing for America Tone briefed him, together with Neilson and Robert Simms, on his plans to raise a French invasion of

Ireland. 'I hope', Tone wrote to Russell a few months later, 'my friend in Lisburne is a good lad and sticks close to his business; diligence and steadiness will do wonders, and I most heartily wish him success'. The object of Teeling's 'business' may be readily surmised.[2]

The Defenders originated in north Armagh in the mid-1780s in response to Peep O'Day Boys raiding Catholic homes, smashing looms and spinning wheels, and searching for firearms. In the eighteenth century the right to bear arms symbolised citizenship even more than the franchise, and so, in effect, the Peep O'Day Boys were unilaterally enforcing the penal law that stripped 'papists' of that right. Defenderism spread gradually along the sectarian fault-lines of mid-Ulster and into the north Leinster border counties, before expanding dramatically in the seismic political turbulence of the early 1790s. Then on 21 September 1795 the low intensity conflict between the Defenders and Peep O'Day Boys, which had persisted in north Armagh throughout this period, erupted into 'The Battle of the Diamond', and resulted in a rout of the Defenders. After the battle the victorious Peep O'Day Boys reconstituted themselves as the Loyal Orange Order, a localised, plebeian, masonic-styled society that soon swelled into a formidable, state-sanctioned, counter-revolutionary force. 'That county has always been a plague to us' observed Russell[3]; and it soon got worse.

In the 'Armagh outrages', which followed the 'Battle of the Diamond', armed bands of Orangemen expelled thousands of Catholics from their homes. Those mass expulsions presented law and order problems in a number of ways. First, the local magistrates proved incapable of preventing the attacks, and secondly, some magistrates and some courts displayed a Protestant partisanship, which made the case against Protestant Ascendancy as eloquently as could any United Irish handbill. In November, McCracken and fellow Belfast United Irishman Joseph Cuthbert posted bond to cover the legal costs of attorney James McGucken in his proceedings against the 'Armagh wreckers'. Further proceedings were later instigated by Bernard Coyle and others, assisted by councillor Henry Joy[4] who shared his cousin McCracken's sense of justice, if not his republican politics. The Insurrection Act of March 1796 disclosed just how politically contaminated the magistrates were and registered the scale of the mounting 'security' crisis. Magistrates were given the power to 'proclaim' their districts, placing them under martial law and indemnifying them against prosecution for any illegal acts they might themselves commit. In effect, as the guardians of the state saw it, the constitution had to be suspended in order to preserve it.

In January 1796 the body of Michael Philips, a Franciscan Friar and informer who had infiltrated the Defenders, was retrieved from a stream near Cromac Dock in Belfast. Several other political assassinations followed, and it is at around this time, according to Neilson's biographer Kenneth Dawson, that Henry Joy McCracken, an otherwise 'attractive and charismatic personality', began 'to exhibit the characteristics of a political fanatic'.[5] Dawson argues elsewhere that 'there is evidence that he was associated with an active programme of removing those engaged in intelligence operations against the United Irishmen', and cites a letter from Mary Ann smuggled into her brother in Kilmainham Gaol in which she refers to

> a certain article which was the only cause of uneasiness to you at the time you were taken up, was concealed in the house till the late strict search which has been made about town, and not daring to keep it any longer, we gave it in charge to a man in whom we had confidence, who buried it in the country so that its being found can't injure any person.

'Long before the days of 21st century forensics,' he concludes, 'the McCrackens were well aware of the need to dispose of the evidence.'[6] Yet Mary Ann also wrote, 'what is morally wrong can never be politically right. Have you not observed that since the assassinations began the cause of the people (which had before been rapidly gaining ground) has gradually declined.'[7]

Henry Joy Jnr, an entirely hostile witness, records the operation of an 'Assassination Committee'; Jemmy Hope, an equally invested witness, not only denied its existence, but declares McCracken's opposition to such killings as did occur.[8] What is clear is that, by their actions, both United Irishmen and state actors were ratcheting up the conflict. On the morning of 26 September 1796 Lord Castlereagh entered the town of Belfast with a detachment of cavalry to conduct the arrest of select United Irish leaders, including Neilson, Russell, Henry Haslett, and Rowley Osborne, formally of the Belfast Jacobins. Again, the intimacy of the Irish political world in this period is striking. As Robert Stewart, the successful popular candidate for County Down in the 1790 general election, Castlereagh knew Neilson personally. Charles Teeling, arrested in Lisburn earlier that day, described him as a 'friend of my father'.[9] The list of names on this 'wanted list' reflected Dublin Castle's current risk assessments, and it is significant where the arrests were (and were not) made. It would have made sense to round up Oliver Bond and others in Dublin, for example. But government agents were focused firmly on the north. They were also acting on reliable intelligence provided by the informer, William Bird. Not that all the activities, or any of the opinions, of the arrested men were precisely covert. Russell sent a copy of his recently published (and probably actionable) pamphlet, *A Letter to the People of Ireland*, to undersecretary Edward Cooke, who sent it back by return of post, because he had read it already.[10]

Henry Joy avoided capture that day, either because he was not in town, or because the warrant was made out for 'James McCracken'.[11] He was subsequently arrested on 10 October and despatched to Dublin to join his fellow state prisoners. The Castle had enough intelligence to detain, but not enough legal-grade evidence to pro-secute and convict the northern leaders. Thus as 'state prisoners' they were charged with treason, but, like later internees, held indefinitely without coming to trial – an extra-legal device retro-actively 'regularised' by the suspension of *Habeas Corpus* on the 26 October 1796. Writing to his sister from Kilmainham Gaol McCracken recommended that she read William Godwin's novel *Caleb Williams* (1794) to gain some understanding of prison life.

'Oh,' proclaims Godwin's protagonist,

> how enviable is the most tottering shed under which the labourer retires to rest, compared with the residence of these walls! . . . the massy doors, the resounding locks, the gloomy passages, the grated windows, and the characteristic looks of the keepers, accustomed to reject every petition, and to steel their hearts against feeling and pity.[12]

The tone of Teeling's description of his arrival in Kilmainham eerily (and perhaps intentionally) echoes Godwin's earlier fictional account,

> It was late when we arrived at this mansion of human misery, under a strong escort of British dragoons. The stillness of the night; the solitary gloom of the prison; the echo of feet as we passed through the long vaulted corridor; the alternate clank of a chain and the grating of the dungeon door, which opened to entomb the victim, were all calculated to inspire sentiments of horror in a man tainted with guilt, or imbued with crime. And was this to be the residence of those whose *crime* was love of country, and whose *guilt* was attachment to the human race?[13]

The great irony is that Kilmainham, which first opened for business in 1796, was a state-of-the-art prison, designed and administered, supposedly, on modern principles of reform and best practice as set out in John Howard's *The State of the Prisons* (1777), and in the British Penitentiary Act of 1779. Long-term incarceration did not become the standard means of punishing or deterring crime until the nineteenth century, and before then the general prison population consisted mostly of those – highwaymen, poachers, debtors, and the like – awaiting either trial or punishment. Sentencing ran from the pillory, flogging, or transportation, to the gibbet, and during the long eighteenth century and the elaboration of the 'Bloody Code' the number of capital offences in Britain rose from about 50 in in 1688 to 'something like 225' by 1814.[14] As in much else, Ireland followed Britain in the execution of 'criminal justice', and in the years 1780 to 1795, for example, 165 of the '199 verified hangings' in Dublin were of felons 'convicted of robbery, burglary, horse theft and other property offences'.[15] Most offenders, however, were transported. Hundreds of alleged 'Defenders', rounded up by Lord Carhampton in and about County Roscommon in the Autumn of 1795 were summarily impressed into the Royal Navy. The comparative rarity of prolonged imprisonment then marked out political prisoners as political. McCracken addressed his smuggled letters from 'the Irish Bastille.'

Howard and the other evangelical reformers identified two major problems in the eighteenth-century British prison. First, the open plan layout that allowed inmates of every sort to mix in promiscuous squalor functioned, in the words of the novelist and magistrate Henry Fielding, as 'seminaries of vice and sewers of nastiness and disease'.[16] And second, the unregulated, unsupervised regime of the jailors, keepers, and turnkeys allowed these sub-contractors of the state to bully and fleece prisoners at will. The solution to the first problem lay in cellularisation which would reduce the risks of bodily and moral infection and increase hygiene by improved daylight and ventilation, whitewashed and limed walls; and thus result in the spiritual cleansing of Christian instruction. Meanwhile the jailors were to be subject to external inspection, made accountable for their behaviour, and prohibited from exacting fees from inmates. Almost none of this happened in McCracken's Kilmainham.

The new prison, built on high ground to benefit from cleaner air, was also designed to provide more light. However, it was also built of limestone, which 'weeps' in damp climates like Dublin's. It did boast cellular 'accommodation' to be sure, but not enough, and it quickly became overcrowded, as did every prison tender and county gaol in the country. Henry Joy, Samuel Neilson, and Charles Teeling, each contracted serious illnesses and over the next 15 months all 3 were eventually bailed on health grounds. In contrast, Thomas Russell became the longest serving state prisoner, spending two years in Newgate, and another four in Fort George, Scotland, before his release in 1802. As for the conduct of the gaolers, the similarities between Godwin's fictional and Teeling's remembered accounts is again arresting. Both catch the injustice visited upon the powerless by the unaccountable: 'their tyranny had no other limit than their caprice. To whom should the unfortunate felon appeal?' writes Godwin; 'caprice' observes Teeling, 'operated on the minds of those in power'. Both likewise condemned the withholding of books, pen, ink, and paper.[17] As to the systemic fleecing of inmates, 'it is expensive to live here', complained McCracken, 'plundered by turnkeys'.[18]

When Mary Ann chided her brother about unused space in his letters, he replied 'indeed there can be very little variety of incident in a jail, one day must be an almost perfect picture of an age when we are shut out from the world. The only rarity that may rise here must be in our own ideas.'[19] To counteract the daily monotony, prisoners had to devise their own entertainment. McCracken liked to play handball when he could. Teeling recounts how

> with much labour and perseverance we succeeded in detaching the locks from our doors, and when our gaolers had retired to rest, and the inmates of the prison were supposed to be in profound repose, we opened our cells and enjoyed that sweet intercourse of society which those only deprived of it can appreciate. We replaced our locks before morning with the same caution but with less labour than we had disengaged them in the night.

Eventually they were discovered leaving their cells. Oliver Bond's wife delivered the prisoners a Christmas pie 'filled with writing materials, foreign and domestic newspapers, [and] communications from friends'.[20]

Teeling understood that the authorities tried to keep the political inmates apart, because 'in society we might plot against the state, and, being of rebellious dispositions encourage insubordination in the prison.'[21] But the intimate camaraderie of prison life is prone to bitter rifts among active men living at close quarters, and in enforced idleness. 'You will say we see the worst side of man in jail' Henry Joy told his sister, 'true, but I did not think he had so bad a side . . . some of the prisoners here are very angry with me, because I took notice of an impropriety . . . in their conduct, [and] they have written to the north about it.'[22] The impropriety referred to Neilson's breach, as McCracken saw it, of a compact made by the first batch of state prisoners that they would only deal with the government collectively. Whether Neilson had in fact broken his word is a moot point. With her husband's health collapsing, and his drinking heavily, Neilson's wife – who was not party to the compact – appealed to government for his release. Mary Ann could see the arguments on both sides of the case and if anything found in favour of Neilson, of whose suffering and sacrifice she reminded her brother. One of his fellow prisoners, Henry Haslett, was so angry at McCracken that he assaulted him with a metal pot.[23] Whatever the right or wrongs of the whole sorry episode, it demonstrates once more the 'steadfastness' of character that would become part of the legend of Henry Joy.

With the flow of information from the outside limited and erratic, McCracken and his comrades could only look on helplessly as events unfolded: the formation of Yeomanry corps, more Protestant, loyal, and more well-healed, than, it was thought, the politically unreliable militia, the arms searches, and the spectre of Orange reaction. Wolfe Tone landed in France in February 1796 to lobby the ruling Directory to launch an invasion of Ireland. McCracken would not have known the detail, but he was highly enough placed in the councils of the United Irishmen to be aware of the thrust. Indeed, in 1795 his older brother Frank had argued against French intervention.[24] Tone's spectacular diplomatic success culminated in the logistical failure and bad luck of a French fleet, some of which reached Bantry Bay in Christmas week, 1796, only to be scattered by a 'Protestant Wind'. If England had had it closest call since the Spanish Armada, the consequences for Ireland were nonetheless momentous.

The near escape at Bantry Bay prompted an influx of new recruits into the ranks of the United Irish movement, afterwards scorned by Jemmy Hope as opportunistic 'foreign aid men', whereas a rattled political establishment responded by intensifying its campaign of repression, known as the 'dragooning of Ulster'. On 13 March 1797, General Lake, commander of Crown forces in the north, issued a proclamation ordering a general surrender of arms, and initiating yet more searches, ransacking of homes, and arrests. Three days later Mary Ann informed her brother of 'six prisoners brought into town this evening, for refusing to swear allegiance and [they] came in undismayed and singing Erin go Brath', and the next month a batch of 19 northerners, among them Henry Joy's older brother William, the Revd Sinclair Kelburn, and a family friend, the weaver, James Burnside, arrived in Kilmainham.[25] Acting on the information of the informer Edward Newell, they were apprehended by Colonel Barber, the commander of the Belfast garrison, who had so memorably crossed paths with McCracken in 1793. On 16 May, in a classic set-piece exercise in state terror, four Monaghan militiamen, court-martialled for swearing the United Irish oath, were executed by firing squad in front of all the duly assembled troops stationed at Blaris camp. Three days later Monaghan militiamen smashed the printing presses of the *Northern Star*.

Overcrowding in the prison, which inevitably resulted from the dragooning of Ulster, aggravated Henry Joy's rheumatism. At one point he shared a damp, cramped cell with four others, and as William McCracken noted, 'when the light of the morning comes we find we have more company than we bargain or wish for, but this I suppose is inseparable from the beds and bedding of gaols.'[26] The brothers were split apart for a time, then reunited, as the pressure on space tightened. With no room left for solitary confinement, and 'surplus' inmates redistributed to makeshift prison ships and military provosts, Dublin's Newgate became known mordantly as 'The Belfast Hotel'.[27]

If, as a prisoner, Henry Joy did not experience directly the worst excesses of Lake's counterinsurgency, their impact upon him can be imagined all the same. In July, for instance, his younger, politically inactive brother John informed him of 'the barbarities committed on the innocent people by the Yeomen and Orangemen'.

The practice among them is to hang a man up by the heels with rope full of twist, by which means the sufferer whirls round like a bird roasting at the fire, during which he is lashed with belts etc., to make him tell where he has concealed arms. Last week, at a place near Dungannon, a young man being used in this manner called to his father for assistance, who being inflamed at the sight struck one of the party a desperate blow with his turf spade; but, alas! his life paid forfeit of his rashness; his entrails were torn out and exposed on a thorn bush.[28]

Undoubtedly, however, the most notorious chapter in the 1797 book of horrors is the hanging on 14 October in Carrickfergus of the United Irishman William Orr. Orr's trial and jurors were legally corrupt and his speech from the scaffold was the stuff that folk legend is made of: 'I am no traitor. I am persecuted for a persecuted country. Great Jehovah receive my soul. I die in the true faith of a Presbyterian'. McCracken was deeply affected and like another non-eyewitness to the bloody events of 1797, Wolfe Tone in France, vowed vengeance. His state of health increasingly precarious, on 9 December 1797 Henry Joy was released on bail, put up by Bernard Coyle, then living in Dublin. He stayed on in the capital for some days before returning home to Belfast. There, fatigued by the strains of prison life, liquid self-medication, and chronic illness, he collapsed.

CHAPTER SIX

Commander in Chief

By the beginning of 1798, when Henry Joy got back on his feet, the United Irish organisation in Ulster, though essentially intact had been depleted and battered by years of fierce repression. The national leadership and centre of gravity of the movement had shifted from Belfast to Dublin. This can be seen, for example, in the replacement of the *Northern Star*, a casualty of the counter-insurgency, by *The Press*, published in Dublin and edited by the former MP from County Cork, Arthur O'Connor. When released from Kilmainham in February Neilson chose to stay in the capital, where the decisions and the plans for insurrection were being made. The leadership divided between those such as O'Connor, Lord Edward Fitzgerald, and Oliver Bond, who advocated unilateral action, and those like Thomas Addis Emmet and William James MacNevin who counselled caution and awaiting French intervention before rising. Neilson naturally aligned himself with the militants. The O'Connor-Fitzgerald faction won the argument and preparations for rebellion proceeded apace, but 'foreign aid' syndrome lingered; not least, as McCracken would discover, in the north. In February McCracken himself met with the Leinster Directory in Dublin to co-ordinate plans for a rising, north and south, and while there visited Russell in Newgate.

The counter-insurgency also moved south during the spring of 1798, and after the rebellion several rebel memoirists – MacNevin,

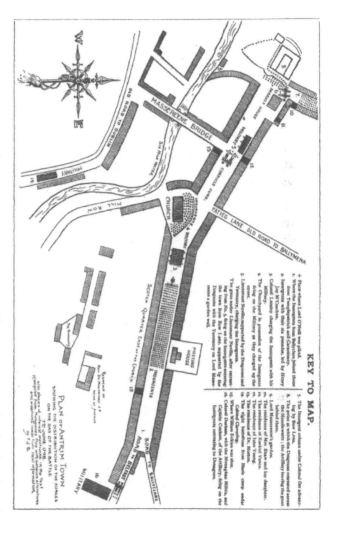

F. J. Bigger, used as an illustration in W. S. Smith 'Memories of '98", in *Ulster Journal of Archaeology*, Second Series, 1:2 (1895), p. 142.

Myles Byrne and Thomas Cloney from Wexford, and Joseph Holt from Wicklow – framed the uprising as a desperate popular response to a savage campaign of repression, to pitch-cappings, house burnings, half-hangings, and an alleged Orange 'extermination oath'. Castlereagh's remark about 'the means taken to explode' rebellion was so often cited, and so assiduously recycled that, over half a century later Karl Marx used it to accuse the government of deliberate provocation.[1] While none of the writers invented the catalogue of outrage perpetrated by crown forces, and repression was undoubtedly a significant cause of rebellion, their interpretation served to deflect responsibility for the conflict away from plotting United Irishmen, and unto the shoulders of ascendancy hardliners, Dublin Castle, and the proverbial 'cowardly Yeomen'. But, as Henry Joy's trips to Dublin in the spring of 1798 suggest, that reading wilfully underestimated the scale and penetration of United Irish organisation, the mass manufacture of pikes, and, in Watty Cox's *Union Star*, the inflammable rhetoric of political assassination. Besides, in an attempt to rally lower-class Catholic support, the United Irishmen probably *did invent* the Orange 'extermination oath'. Nevertheless, it is the case that in the run in to rebellion the United Irish leadership sustained a series of lethal blows, which weakened national and provincial co-ordination, and lent credence to the legend of 1798 as a spontaneously combusting, chaotic, *jacquerie*.

On 10 March, a detachment of troops led by Town Major, Henry Sirr raided a meeting of the Leinster Directory in Oliver Bond's Bridge Street home in Dublin. Delegates from Queen's County, and from counties Meath, Kildare, and Carlow were arrested, as were others elsewhere in the city, including Emmet and MacNevin. The organisation's military commander, Lord Edward, went into hiding. On 30 March the privy council issued a proclamation declaring Ireland to be in rebellion and placing the country under martial law. Back in Dublin in mid-May, McCracken reported that 'the people expect to have the soldiers living at free quarters'[2]. Six days later on 18 May Lord Edward was fatally wounded resisting arrest. The rebellion began as planned on the night of the 23 May. Counties Meath and Kildare saw rebel actions, but crucially, a heavily garrisoned Dublin remained firmly under government control.

The decimation of the United Irish leadership, and its utter inability to erect and man the barricades in the streets of the capital city, had devastating consequences for the progress of the insurrection. The United Irish project began in Belfast, and the men who gathered with Wolfe Tone on Cave Hill in 1795 – Neilson, McCracken, Russell, and Simms – had directed that project's revolutionary 'new departure'. Now, as south Wicklow and Wexford erupted, the north continued to hesitate. On 1 June Robert Simms resigned as Adjutant General for Antrim.[3] Over the next two days the Ulster Directory debated what course of action it should take. McCracken advocated taking the field, against a majority who wanted to hold back until the arrival of the French. McCracken succeeded Simms as Adjutant General for Antrim, but only two of the twenty-three Antrim colonels declared for action.[4] On 5 June William Steel Dickson, Adjutant General for County Down was arrested, and McCracken now succeeded him too, becoming Commander in Chief for Ulster.

The decision of Simms and of the colonels can be read either as tantamount to desertion, or as a rational choice based on the hard facts on the ground. Their organisation was still recovering from the 'dragooning of Ulster' in the previous year. Belfast and – the strategic and symbolic prize – Dublin were under close military lock-down. What were the chances of success? The Revd Edward Hudson, a keen-eyed loyalist from Portglenone in south Antrim, grasped the rebel quandary, writing to Charlemont on 2 June, the very day the Directory met:

that we are perfectly quiet, is true; that a great number of guns (such as they are) come in daily, is also true. And yet my lord I am not satisfied with the state and disposition of the country. The northerns are indeed wiser and understand calculation better than the people of Kildare and Wicklow; and yet I fear they were very lately on the brink of the precipice over which the others have fallen.[5]

Jemmy Hope, of course, discerned neither wisdom nor tactical 'calculation'. Blending class analysis, hindsight, and conspiracy theory, he blamed spies and foreign aid-men, rich farmers and shopkeepers for the defections, confusions, and betrayals, in the days preceding the battle of Antrim. Only Henry Joy, notes Hope, showing characteristic regard, 'observed the design and operation of this underplot'.[6]

In the first days of the rebellion McCracken proposed taking hostage army officers attending a concert in the Belfast Assembly rooms, a proposition prudently rejected as the town turned rapidly into a military-security complex.[7] The Poor House and the south side of the White Linen Hall were converted into temporary barracks.[8] After his capture Henry Joy was initially held prisoner in the Donegall Arms, scene in more hopeful times to much Volunteer toasting and dining for Ireland, and later tried in the Exchange, a symbol of late eighteenth-century Belfast's commercial and civic vigour. The town was proclaimed, guarded, patrolled, searched, and curfewed. One night, Colonel Barber 'surprised a committee of 33 people, assembled at the Sign of the White Cross [tavern]in Pottinger's Entry, and lodged them prisoners'. They belonged in fact to a combination of journeyman tailors (or illegal trade union). Other less fortunate prisoners were marched in daily from the surrounding countryside. A townsman, John Kelso, was sentenced to 800 – and received 200 –lashes for concealing arms.[9] Hope was in Belfast on the day Kelso and others were flogged, recalling that 'it was strongly guarded by the military at every entrance; it was easy to get in, but how to get out was another question.' 'A comrade' of his did however manage to smuggle out two swords, a green jacket, and the colours which, days later, flew at the Battle of Antrim.[10]

Henry Joy McCracken issued his general orders:

> Army of Ulster, tomorrow we march on Antrim; drive the garrison of Randalstown before you and haste to form a junction with the Commander in Chief.
>
> Ist Year of Liberty, 6th day of June, 1798.

There are a number of deftly crafted modern narrative accounts of the battle that ensued, but that shrewd contemporary observer of events, Edward Hudson, provides a useful reminder that there can only ever be *versions* of the past, some of which, of course, are more persuasive, more reliable, than others. 'To attempt giving an accurate account of what has passed in this country,' he reflected, 'would be like sitting down to draw a picture of chaos', before, interestingly, going on to challenge the fidelity of the official record. 'I had three accounts of it from persons who were present, and they might pass for accounts of three battles fought in different parts of the globe.'[11] One small episode demonstrates that *Rashomon* principle in action. As the rebel army marched on the town of Antrim they sang *La Marseillaise,* accompanied, according to Charles Teeling, by bugle and fife, or, according to the traditional song 'Henry Joy', by fife and drum, or, according to Jemmy Hope's distant recollection, absent 'musical instruments of any kind'.[12] Detail matters, but contradictory detail does not grant an historical licence to wander around, lost in the fog of war – better rather to cut an imperfect narrative route through 'the bloody meadow'.

In an echo of his earlier plan to take army officers hostage in Belfast, Henry Joy targeted Antrim town in hopes of capturing the county governor, Lord John O'Neill, and county magistrates assembled there. Four rebel army contingents were to converge on the town, one from the south on the Belfast Road, under the command of Henry Joy, one from the Randalstown area to the west, led by Samuel Orr, brother of the United Irish martyr, William, one from the Kells area to the north, and finally a forth from the east on the Carrickfergus Road. This was dense United Irish territory, and many thousand citizen soldiers were 'out' that day, up to 4000 of them gathering on Donegore Hill alone, and there were minor engagements in the coastal towns of Larne and Glenarm. Critically, the Defenders, notionally 7000 strong, did not turn up, certainly not *en bloc*, for the fight – a breach of faith that caused bitter post-rebellion recriminations.[13]

Henry Joy raised the green standard of rebellion at Roughfort and his 500 or so mostly Killead and Templepatrick men set out in high spirts and good order, marching in three 'divisions', musketeers to the front (Jemmy Hope's 'Spartan Band'), then the main body of pikemen, and taking up the rear a smaller complement equipped with a light field piece, mounted on a common country cart. The cannon had been hidden in the Templepatrick meeting house at the time of the suppression of the Volunteers earlier in the decade, and unlike several other light artillery secreted in Belfast and environs, had escaped detection. The traces of Volunteer experience indicated by the cannon, 'the great spirit' and, in the words of a loyalist account, 'steadiness', of the rebel advance into the High Street of Antrim at around 2.30 p.m. on 7 June, show that for the moment an elementary military discipline, and chain of command, held.[14] But the lack of military training, flimsy planning, and inexperience of combat, soon told, as on the enemy side the loose discipline of militia conscripts, the gentleman amateurishness of the Yeomanry, and the combat innocence of the fencibles, all added to the disarray. Regular dragoons, cavalry, and artillery, did in the end prove decisive, and yet, it was later claimed, 'no officer commanding a detachment has any orders how to act when attacked, nor is there any communication between the different detachments . . . the officers commanding have not a single order or instruction during the whole time of alarm'.[15]

Entering the town, the Unitedmen came under heavy musket fire from a company of light dragoons on a lane near the church-yard, and hails of grapeshot from a fieldpiece in the churchyard itself, which commanded the main street. Their own cannon mal-functioned, but the Spartan Band gained the churchyard, relieving the pikemen, and after an hour's fierce fighting the insurgents took control of the town, except for Lord Massarene's demesne at the end of the High Street, from whose 30 foot wall Yeomen kept up fire on the rebels below. Meanwhile, General Nugent, fully apprised of McCracken's design by a gaggle of informers, had despatched reinforcements: Lord Donegall's Yeomanry corps, dragoons, and artillery, from Belfast, under the command of Colonel Durham, and dragoons, Argyle fencibles, and Monaghan militia, from Blaris, under the command of Colonel Clavering. As Clavering's forced-marching troops approached Antrim, the cavalry raced ahead.

Entering the town, the cavalry, led by Colonel Lumley, mounted a Tennysonian charge, and were hacked to bits by a phalanx of pikemen at the churchyard, and by crossfire from musketeers who had occupied buildings on either side of the High Street. Lord O'Neill, for whom, as John O'Neill, old Francis Joy had voted in 1790, was fatally wounded in the first 'rash and unfortunate charge', as, upon a second attempt, was Lumley himself, whose 'cool intrepidity and manly conduct' won 'the admiration of the contending ranks'.[16] A regimental history records that 5 officers and 47 men were slain 'in a few minutes'.[17] Clavering's infantry had

still a mile to go before reaching the town, but any advantages the
rebels might have earned by repulsing Lumley's dragoons were
instantly squandered. At the moment they arrived on the scene of
battle, the 500 or so men who had, as instructed, driven the garrison
of Randalstown before them, mistaking cavalry in retreat for a
cavalry charge, broke ranks and fled.

Durham's forces cannonaded the town from high ground,
while advancing Yeomen surrounded some rebels 'stationed' in a
field 'and slaughtered them without mercy'.[18] On the High Street
panic turned retreat into rout; only the Spartan Band withdrawing
in good order. 'But this is one of the disputed points'.[19] According
to the loyalist historian, Samuel McSkimin, dragoons from Blaris
arrived 'bringing with them some thirty prisoners whom they had
taken by the way, with arms in their hands . . . [who] were disposed
of in a very summary manner, as were such wounded as were found
about the gardens and streets.' That night Monaghan militia
returning to Blaris burned down the village of Templepatrick,
'because the insurgents had hidden several pieces of cannon in the
meeting house'.[20]

The remnants of the defeated army made for the camp on
Donegore Hill, but there too panic had wreaked havoc. 'Upon
notice of their defeat at Antrim', reported the *Belfast News-Letter*,
the Donegore men 'began to disperse, and their numbers were
reduced from betwixt 2000 and 3000 to 30 or 40 . . . in a very short
time'. Abandoned pikes littered the roadsides and ditches.[21] In the
lines of the 'weaver poet' James Orr,

> The *camp's* brak up. Owre braes, an' bogs,
> The *patriots* seek their *sections*;
> Arms, ammunition, bread-bags, brogues,
> Lye skail'd in a' directions[22]

A combatant's description of the rising in County Down, which began at Saintfield on 9 June, and culminated in the battle of Ballynahinch on 13 to 14 June, fits Antrim equally well.

> Instead of the [republican] forces meeting at any point in collected and organised bodies, they met rather more by accident than design, and they were in no better order than a country mob . . . when thus assembled, without provisions, without officers, and without military subordination.[23]

Turning from the shambolic spectacle on Donegore Hill McCracken and about 100 of his more stalwart followers, including Hope, set out for Ballymena, believing it to be still 'in the hands of the people'.[24] With Clavering and some 400 troops on their trail, the bedraggled and exhausted rump of the rebel army then diverted to Slemish mountain, and there camped on its slopes as night closed in on 7 June, 'the 1st year of liberty', 1798.

CHAPTER SEVEN

'Faithful to the last'

Colonel Clavering sent the fugitives on Slemish an ultimatum, demanding that they hand over four named leaders, each with a 100 guinea price on his head, and in return the rest would be spared His Majesty's retribution. The insurgents made a counter-offer of a 400 guinea reward for bringing Clavering to justice.[1] The red coats stalled, however, because their commander had apparently overestimated the strength of the enemy, and McCracken's remnant quietly dispersed. McCracken, Hope and a handful of others struck out southward towards the Belfast mountains. Living 'on the run', on the night of 13 June they reached 'the height of Little Collin', from where they saw the flames of burning houses in north Down, and could hear the distant rumble of cannon fire from the battle of Ballynahinch.[2] And whereas Henry Joy Jnr 'clearly recollect[ed] the death-like silence which pervaded the streets when the counties of Down and Antrim resounded with the noise of tumult of battle', the *News-Letter* at the time reported that 'cannonading was distinctly heard in this town'.[3] Indeed the columns of the *News-Letter* were packed with reports about troop movements, courts martial, and the daily arrival of fresh batches of prisoners, side by side with advertisements placed by terrified local communities, including the inhabitants of Killead, professing their loyalty, and repudiating rebellion by deluded people duped by traitors. McCracken tried to avoid the post-rebellion frenzy by literally staying above it, crossing over to Divis mountain, and holing up in a (comparatively) remote, disused cabin on Black Bohall.

In coming to a rest at Bohall, also rendered Bowhill, or The Bohill, McCracken almost certainly acted on local knowledge, topographical and political. For the people around this poor, high scrubland – 'Hannahstown' – were the poor descendants of the native Clandeboye and *Béal Feirste* Catholics dispossessed by plantation. In a word, they were the stuff Defenderism is made of. McCracken would also have been known to the Presbyterian inhabitants of the Knockcairn-Glenavy area, a few miles to the west of the Belfast mountains, where he set up a short-lived calico works in 1795. From his 'lodging in the open air' he wrote to Mary Ann, in words that entered Irish republican tradition. Antrim had been lost, he told her, 'entirely owning to treachery, *the rich always betray the poor.*'[4] To use the vernacular of literary theory, that sentence merits some 'unpacking'. The treachery and betrayal refer to informers and deserters, and 'the rich' to the strong farmers and shopkeepers castigated by Hope, and to the merchant and manufacturing class, from which McCracken himself came.

The figure of the informer is a stock character in Irish nationalist and republican folklore. As James Joyce's Stephen Dedalus remarks to his 'advanced' nationalist friend Davin in *Portrait of the Artist as a Young Man*, 'when you make the next rebellion with hurleysticks . . . and want the indispensable informer, tell me. I can find you a few in this college.' Looking back on 1798, Charles Teeling reflected 'the spy and informer have always faced encouragement in the bloody annals of Ireland's distress; but in the present period, there was a systematic arrangement of villainy and fraud . . . regarded with horror by their fellow-Irishmen.'[5] From start to finish the United Irish movement was rotten with informers, readymade villains who probably provide a too easy explanation for operational failures, but in the case of Antrim at least, treachery did play a lethal hand. Well before McCracken raised the standard of rebellion at Roughfort, General Nugent in Belfast was well informed about his destination. When Henry Joy issued his orders to the reluctant colonels, each in command of 500 men, some of them promptly passed on their instructions to the general. 'We were betrayed at all points,' writes Hope, and more cryptically, 'Simms concealed the signal'.[6]

Hope viewed the traitors as 'foreign aid men'; petit bourgeois, who had signed on for revolution as soon as, but not before, the appearance of a French fleet in Bantry Bay raised the prospect of success, but the mention of Simms, a wealthy merchant, is intriguing. The United Irishmen were fiercely anti-aristocracy, disdaining its inherited privilege and political power, social hauteur, and retinues of servile hangers-on, whereas the leadership were themselves largely bourgeois, businessmen, lawyers, printers, and clergy. As we have seen, one of the most radical among them, Thomas Russell, exempted commercial wealth from his strictures on economic inequality and injustice. Yet Hope recalled a conversation he once had with McCracken, the son of a sea captain and merchant, about 'shipping interests and commercial establishments' – 'well' said I, 'Harry, there are men that will put the rope on your neck and mine, if ever they get us into their power'.[7] Sometimes 'the rich' just meant the rich.

Mary Ann McCracken with her sister in law, Williams's wife Rose Ann, again probably with the help of local connections, tracked her brother down, bringing clothes, food, and news, and opening lines of communication to his family, and to his comrades still at liberty. Mary Ann then returned on a second occasion, when McCracken was staying in the cottage of a gamekeeper, David Bodle, the father of Mary, and, wholly unknown to Mary Ann, mother of Henry Joy's daughter, Maria. The supplies she delivered that day included a copy of Edward Young's long poem 'Night Thoughts', sent by their mother.[8] The full original title of Stewart

Parker's 1984 play is *Northern Star, (or McCracken's Night Thoughts)*, and in it the Mary Ann character comments acidly on Young's verse, 'Ten thousand lines of sanctimonious gush. Spiritual consolation she calls it. I told her you had no need of such nonsense.'[9] But this is the voice of Parker, not of the historical Mary Ann. The twentieth-century playwright refused (while this twenty-first-century historian failed) to make the imaginative leap into the eighteenth-century sensibility. It *is* hard to imagine how a man in imminent danger of capture and death might find comfort in a poem which mediates 'on Life, Death, and Immortality: in nine nights'. As darkness falls at the end of the first stanza, Young asks:

> Fate! Drop the curtain; I can lose no more.
> How much is to be done! My hopes and fears
> Start up alarm'd and o'er life's narrow verge
> Look down – on what?

And so it goes on:

> A dread eternity! How surely *mine*!
> How populous, how vital is the grave!
> Death! Great proprietor of all![10]

However, this 'period piece' as it now seems, was highly esteemed by, for example, Boswell and Coleridge, who admired its exquisite 'feeling' and Christian certitude. So, perhaps it should not be too much of a stretch after all, to imagine Henry Joy, a man of his times, finding consolation in Young's sense of assured salvation.[11] As his friend Russell confided to his journal 'let all men look only hereafter for their rewards and then the gu[il]lotine will have no terrors.'[12]

McCracken, whose encounters with the condemned in Kilmainham induced 'a sort of carelessness about death', also said

that he had no 'desire to die of sickness'.[13] But this states a
preference for being killed in the field, not an indifference to being
hanged. Through his contacts he secured a passage to America on
a ship anchored in Belfast Lough. After spending the night in a
safe house in the townland of Greencastle, on 7 July – one month
to the day, since the battle of Antrim – Henry Joy, posing as a car-
penter, and two companions, Gawen [or Garvin] Watt, and John
Query, a bookbinder by trade, were stopped on the road by a party of
Yeoman, one of whom recognised McCracken. They were arrested
and committed immediately to the county gaol in Carrickfergus.[14]
There he was held for just over a week, visited by Mary Ann and
his father, before being taken to Belfast, where the unfolding
drama played out with human intimacy, and in small town detail.
On 16 July Henry Joy was first lodged in the Donegall Arms,
tavern turned makeshift prison, in Castle Place, then, witnessed by
Mary Ann, marched to the artillery barracks at the bottom of Ann
Street. Mary Ann asked Colonel Durham – who had bombarded
Antrim – to grant the family access to her brother. He refused, and
she then searched out Colonel Barber – who had been confronted
on the street by Henry Joy five years before – dining in the
Exchange with fellow officers, and he granted permission.[15]
Perhaps he respected the character of an adversary whose politics
he deplored.

Next day the court martial took place, also in the Exchange,
near Sugar House Entry, and Peggy Barclay's tavern, once a
clearing house for United Irish gossip, plotting, and recruitment.
After a brisk trial, prosecuted by the crown attorney, John Pollock,
and a perfunctory identification provided by two random 'witnesses',
Henry Joy was sentenced to death for treason and rebellion, and
returned to the barracks. Mary Ann and his father (but not his
mother) attended the proceedings, and now joined him in his
condemned cell. Pollock entered and offered McCracken a deal. In

return for naming the Antrim commander, who had resigned on 1 June, the sentence of execution would be commuted to banishment. Henry Joy answered that he 'would do anything which his father knew it was right for him to do'. 'Harry, my dear', said Captain McCracken, 'I know nothing of the business, but you know best what you ought to do.' 'Farewell, then father,' he replied.[16]

Mary Ann, the bringer of Edward Young's 'Night Thoughts', long after recollected:

we had been brought up in the firm conviction of an all-wise and overruling Providence, and of the duty of entire resignation to the Divine Will. I remarked that his death was as much a dispensation of Providence as if it had happened in the common course of nature, to which he assented.[17]

Henry Joy was attended in his last hours by the Revd Steel Dickson, the captured commander of County Down, and by Sinclair Kelburn, minister to his own Third Belfast congregation, and his companion in the Volunteers, United Irishmen, and Kilmainham Gaol. It was Dickson, reportedly, who McCracken told about his daughter, Maria, and who in turn told Mary Ann.[18] In the event Maria was adopted by the McCracken family and reared by Mary Ann.

The town major, William Fox, took a locket of Henry Joy's hair from his sister, declaring that 'too much use had already been made of such things.'[19] Mindful perhaps of the popular currency of William Orr's recent political martyrdom – McCracken himself wore a commemorative ring – Fox rightly sensed the danger of secular relics being put into circulation. The authorities were likewise careful to prevent funeral displays, or the turning of graves into patriot shrines. Public executions were highly ritualised affairs, requiring a sort of audience participation, and an assigned 'performance' by those about to be 'launched into eternity'.

However, the theatrical and symbolic impact of political executions could rebound. Nowadays the term 'terrorism' is applied almost exclusively to non-state actors, but in the eighteenth century it was more usually associated with state practice. In fact, the *Oxford English Dictionary Based on Historical Principles* defines terrorism in the first instance as 'government by intimidation as directed and carried out by the party in power in France during the Revolution of 1789–94; the system of the 'Terror' (1793–94).' The High Tory scourge of capital punishment, Samuel Johnson, noted 'the desire of investing lawful authority with terror and governing by force rather than persuasion', while for some historians and theorists the spectacle of public execution virtually defines the eighteenth-century state.[20] When Henry Joy stepped onto the gallows, he stepped, in effect, onto a stage – and he well understood the role he was called upon to play.

Hangings served, or at least were intended to serve, several purposes: to punish the miscreant and deter the criminal, to display power, inspire terror, and to entertain the rabble – in November 1798 Lord Cavan expressed his 'hope' that the execution of Wolfe Tone would 'amuse Dublin'.[21] Yet the extent to which hanging did actually terrorize or deter is open to question. As 'A Magistrate' complained in the *Hibernian Journal* in 1781, the frequency of public executions 'renders them familiar; and the mob seems no more affected by the solemn scene, than [by] a puppet show'.[22] As to deterrence, pickpockets routinely plied their trade in crowds gathered to witness the hanging of their fellow pickpockets.[23] Dr Johnson observed that 'to equal robbery with murder is to reduce murder to robbery, to confound in common minds the gradations of iniquity.'[24] The promiscuous resort to the hangman's noose had, in other words, trivialised capital punishment; political offenders, styled traitors, were therefore subject to more condign and exemplary retribution.

As he passed through Manchester on his way to Scotland in 1759 Benjamin Franklin saw the severed heads of Jacobite traitors still – 13 years after the Battle of Culloden – impaled on spikes outside the town Exchange.[25] As Henry Joy McCracken marched to the gallows on that warm summer's afternoon, 17 July 1798, he beheld the flies swarming around the severed heads of James Dickey, attorney, Crumlin (executed 25 June), John Storey, printer, Belfast (29 June), and Henry Byers (11 July), impaled on spikes in front of the Market House. Byers stood convicted of stealing a bullock from the loyalist squire, Nicholas Price's, farm to help supply the rebel army before the battle of Ballynahinch. The court martial, however, deferred the sentence to Price, who not only called for the death penalty, but accompanied Byers to the scaffold, placing one hand upon his shoulder, pointing with the other to the severed heads, and telling him 'to take heart and go boldly for he should soon have plenty of his neighbours to keep him company.'[26] The fate of another prisoner, the blacksmith Robert Patterson, who shot another of Price's bullocks and requisitioned a pair of his britches, is not recorded.[27] In his *Historical Collections Relative to the Town of Belfast* (1817) Henry Joy Jnr lists the executions in the summer of 1798, including Hugh Grimes, or Graham (6 July), whose body, for reason unknown was spared decapitation, but the hanging of his cousin Henry Joy McCracken is recorded without comment – for reasons that are painfully transparent.[28]

The state always risked losing control of the narrative of public execution; a fine line divided just punishment for treason from political martyrdom, and the condemned knew it. In the last few years of their short lives Henry Joy and his comrades lived consciously in the shadow of the scaffold. As Wolfe Tone reflected in his journal, 'if I become not the gallows as well as another, a plague on my growing up . . . my life is of little consequence, and I should hope not to lose it neither.'[29] Russell reacted with dismay to reports of a renegade French general's last moments on the guillotine block: 'hear of Custine's being executed and his terrors. Much sho[c]ked at it. I thought he would suffer but his irresolution is strange. A man who braved death in the field to be so timid on the scaffold . . . I am continually more affected than by anything I have long heard. Such inconsistency!'[30]

Mary Ann later recalled an exchange around 1793 reiterating that frame of mind:

> If you fail you will lose your lives.
> Henry Joy: whether we fail or succeed we expect to be the first to fall.
> Russell: but of what consequence are our lives or the lives of a few individuals, compared to the liberty and happiness of Ireland?[31]

As their subsequent actions testify, none of this was mere bravado or a casual death wish. When arrested in November, 1798, coming ashore from a captured French frigate at Buncrana, County Donegal, Tone addressed Sir George Hill – whom he knew from their college days – 'with as much sang froid as you might expect'.[32] An Adjutant General in the army of the French Republic, he later slit his own throat rather than suffer the indignity of being hanged as a traitor. In 1803 Russell – defended in his trial by councillor Joy – is said to have placed the noose around his neck with his own hands.[33]

Henry Joy McCracken met his fate in the market square, before the citizens of Belfast and in the words of the song the redcoats mustered there with a resolution rising to the occasion. 'On the scaffold,' wrote Charles Hamilton Teeling,

> he evinced the firmness which he displayed in the field . . . few had better opportunities than myself of estimating the qualities of McCracken. He was my fellow prisoner for twelve months, and often

the companion of my cell. Lively, generous, and sincere, I met no man
who bore privations with greater firmness.[34]

Upon General Nugent's instruction McCracken was not
decapitated, and indeed some weeks before, Martha McTier
informed her brother, Dr Drennan, that 'Nugent is much liked
and always was in this town, and I believe in my soul will act with
all the forbearance the nature and difficulty of his situation will
allow'.[35] The body was handed over to Mrs Burnside, mother of
James, another Kilmainham comrade of Henry Joy's, on the condition that it be buried quickly, quietly, and with plain Christian
ceremony. No less than lockets of dead men's hair, funerals requir-
ed close policing. Burnside and others brought the body to the
McCracken family home in nearby Rosemary street, where a
family doctor attempted forlornly to revive the corpse. As night
fell Henry Joy's mortal remains were buried in St George's
churchyard, located on the south east corner of the High Street,
just a few buildings away from the house where he had been born.

More than Teeling, and as much even as Mary Ann, it is Jemmy
Hope who seeded the legend of his friend and commander, a
protestant dissenter, the 'idol of the poor', and a republican: 'when
all our leaders deserted us,' he wrote, 'Henry Joy McCracken stood
alone, faithful to the last.'[36]

CHAPTER EIGHT

Remembering Henry Joy

And, whatever can be said of the Scots Irish down the centuries, they cannot be accused of having short memories.

- Rory Fitzpatrick, *God's Frontiersmen*.

Henry Joy – People do forget though. They forget the facts that don't suit them.

Mary Anne – They forget nothing in this country, not ever.

- No. It isn't true to say they forget nothing. It's far worse than that. They misremember everything.

- Stewart Parker, *Northern Star*.

No statues raised for Henry Joy.

- Ian McBride, 'Memory and Forgetting'.[1]

For more than a century the remains of Henry Joy McCracken were consigned to an unmarked grave, in a burial ground closed in 1800 as a hazard to public health.[2] Certainly no one thought to go look for him. In contrast to the severed heads of the Manchester Jacobites, or to Oliver Cromwell, whose skull ornamented a spike on Westminster Hall for 24 years, in Belfast's Cornmarket the heads of Dickey, Storey, and Byers, were taken down within weeks on 17 August, 1798.[3] The promptness is congruent with the Lord Lieutenant and Commander in Chief, Marquess Cornwallis's attempts to ratchet down the savagery of post-Rebellion loyalist backlash.[4] Gawen Watt and John Query, who were captured with

Henry Joy, were banished. Frank McCracken fled to America, although he had returned to Ireland by 1803, the year in which his father died. William was arrested but held only briefly before release. He died in the same year as his mother, 1814.[5] Mary Bodle too seems to have gone to America. Edward Bunting continued for decades to collect 'The ancient music of Ireland'; he died in 1843. In 1809 Jemmy Hope, who died in 1847, named his first-born son Henry Joy McCracken Hope. Mary Ann, who had stood by Thomas Russell in 1803, and who raised her niece Maria as her own, died in 1866, at 96 years of age.

I once asked the woman serving behind the bar in The Crosskeys Inn, which is situated in the townland of Ardnaglass, mid-way between Portglenone and Toome in south County Antrim, and which opened for business in 1654, if it is true, as I had heard, that Henry Joy McCracken used to drink there. The historical geography of Defenderism makes this a plausible story, but her answer was an unhesitating and definite: 'no'. How could she be so certain? 'Because if he had, I would know about it.' This is an interesting, and not entirely unreasonable, standard of historical evidence. But, she continued, we do have a picture of his sister, if you'd like to see that. I had, of course, seen reproductions of the Victorian-era photograph many times, and this was a nineteenth-century print, picturing Mary Ann in old age, dressed in bonnet and fittingly fine 'drapery', looking to camera over her spectacles with what – in a piquant gush of regional 'essentialism' – A. T. Q. Stewart called 'her shrewd Ulster eyes'. It is both a striking and an appealing image to be sure, and yet it is suggestive that from the rich horde of iconic figures in the Irish republican tradition the proprietor of the Crosskeys chose Miss McCracken. Perhaps there is something to the tale I was told after all?

The story of Mary Ann is intertwined with, but much more than, that of her brother (who today knows the name of Wolfe

Tone's sister?). By any measure a remarkable woman, to date one of the most substantial treatments of Henry Joy's life is still to be found in Mary McNeill's *The Life and Times of Mary Ann McCracken, 1770-1866 a Belfast Panorama* (1960). An admirer of Mary Wollstonecraft, Mary Ann was a feminist, *avant la lettre*; writing to her brother in Kilmainham that 'there can be no argument produced in favour of the slavery of women that has not been used in favour of general slavery'.[6] She loved Russell, never married, and lived out her long independent life in the best commercial, charitable, and philanthropic traditions of the Joy and McCracken families. Like Russell a staunch abolitionist, she abstained from the consumption of sugar, a product of slave labour in the Americas. As the main character in a Glenn Patterson novel, set in nineteenth-century Belfast, wryly remarks, 'it is said of her that she could not stand still for more than two minutes in one place without a committee forming around her'.[7]

Mary Ann remained steadfastly devoted to the memory of her brother and in the early 1840s handed over copies of Henry Joy's correspondence to the historian (and fellow abolitionist), Richard Robert Madden, then embarking on his multi-volume *The United Irishmen: Their Lives and Times*. Together with Jemmy Hope's memoir also written at this time at the historian's behest, the acquisition of the letters secured McCracken's proper place in Madden's literary pantheon of '98.[8] Documentation – print, and written records of every sort, in a word 'the archive', is the ineluctable staple of historical research. There are of course other traces, visual and archaeological, left by the past; and in the case of folklore and popular memory, oral tradition, that qualify as evidence upon which versions of the past may be constructed. Of these, tradition is perhaps the most difficult to excavate and to verify. However, Samuel McSkimin's *Annals of Ulster, or Ireland Fifty Years Ago*, does contain a glinting little nugget of 'evidence', compacting vernacular-historiographic, visual, archaeological, and local-traditional matter concerning Henry Joy. A collector of oral history, and former Yeoman, he records that a 'small party of McCracken's continued several days in the vicinity of Slemish, and in a marshy spot beneath the southern brow of the mountain they dug a well called by their leader's name, and on some stones adjoining are still seen his initials and those of some of his followers.'[9] Although the *Annals* were published in 1849, McSkimin died in 1843 – the year in which the 79-year old Hope wrote up his living testimony.

By the 1840s the political climate had shifted enough to allow a public reckoning with 1798 – unimaginable in the immediate aftermath of the rebellion. Madden's reclamation project stepped in tune to 'The memory of the dead (Who fears to speak of '98)', a poem, soon after adapted as a ballad, written by a Trinity student, John Kells Ingram, and published, again in 1843, in the Young Irelander, Protestant intellectual, Thomas Davis's paper, *The Nation*. Although never himself a nationalist or republican, Kells Ingram nonetheless enjoined:

Then here's their memory - may it be
For us a guiding light
To cheer our strife for liberty,
And teach us to unite!

But back in the late summer of 1798, and for decades to come, they were all loyalists then. In the 1830s Ordnance Survey fieldworkers in the Antrim and Down sites of rebellion noted of tight-lipped local communities that 'the examples of hangings of them gave them a distaste for such proceedings and has since then had a salutary effect on them, besides effecting a total change in their political sentiments'.[10] The detailed topography of historically recent events remained undisclosed to nosey strangers, and while it is undoubtedly true that the communal trauma of 1798 induced public silences and defused radical politics, the eager Ordnance Surveyors probably failed to also recognise 'the famous northern reticence' of a people who subscribe to the maxim 'whatever you say, say nothing'.[11]

Contemporary memoir likewise rationed and filtered politically delicate information. Thus in *A Narrative of the Confinement and Exile of William Steel Dickson D. D.* (1812), Dickson, the only Presbyterian minister to be held among the state prisoners in Fort George (1799–1802), helpfully explains that before his arrest in early June, 1798, 'I may have been a General, for aught that appears to the contrary; and I may not have been a General, though people said I was. But be that as it was, General, or no General . . .'[12] Charles Teeling's *History of the Irish Rebellion of 1798: A Personal Narrative* (1828) is not quite so slippery, but he too stops well short of full disclosure. Still, his book retains considerable historical value, including perhaps the earliest instalment of the McCracken legend in print. By Teeling's account the 'gallant' McCracken, as prisoner, and as commander in the field, displayed firmness, intelligence, and courage; 'bold and daring', he 'possessed . . . all that energy of soul which is the inseparable companion of the noble mind'.[13] This is also how Henry Joy would be remembered by Hope in the 1840s, and re-remembered by Madden then and in the subsequent editions of the *Lives and Times* over the following years.

Madden focussed on leading United Irishmen, and on middle-ranking figures like Hope, and William Putnam McCabe, whereas antiquaries and collectors of local lore tapped the testimony of the unsung foot soldier such as James Burns, who fought at Antrim, and of orally transmitted 'memory' generally. For example, the Francis Joseph Bigger papers contain a statement by William J, McKinney, dated 7 November, 1904 about his grandfather John, who was 'out' in 1798, based on the information of 'an old man named Jamie Bell who lived near Roughfort', and of 'John Corsby, who was an old brother of Turlough MacSwiney's wife's father, [who] told me that he saw my grandfather galloping past his house three times on the day of the Battle of Antrim'.[14] If that kind of story does not pass the contemporary documentation test of 'what actually happened' history, it is nevertheless essential to the history of how legends are made.

The Presbyterian minister, Classon Emmet Porter, a nephew of the executed Presbyterian minister, and author of *Billy Bluff*, James Porter, began collecting the 'witness statements' of '98 veterans, again in the 1840s – the decade in which the word 'folklore' was coined. In 1863 James Burns, and (at an unspecified date) 'old Malcolm Fleming', who 'told me he saw him [Henry Joy] riding in, dressed with green sashes', both confirmed McSkimin's tale about 'McCracken's Well' at the foot of Slemish. Much of the material collected by Porter appears in R. M. Young's *Ulster in '98* (1893), including the words of a ballad, 'McCracken's Ghost', recited from memory by the 91-year-old Burns.[15] Once more the question almost proposes itself: why, in subaltern culture, is Henry Joy remembered better than other, equally deserving, candidates?

When Young published his book in the 1890s, however, most in protestant Ulster were pledged to forgetting Henry Joy and his traitorous ilk. The very name United Irishmen responds to the blight of sectarian division in Irish politics and society, and it is one of the great and tragic ironies of Irish history that a movement dedicated to the union of 'Protestant, Catholic, and dissenter', in effect contributed to the escalation of sectarian conflict. The actions of the Wexford rebels in particular – the burning of, mostly pro-testant, civilians in Scullabogue barn, the executions on Wexford bridge – were seized upon by government and loyalists to depict the insurrection as a 1641-style papist massacre, and worked into

Sir Richard Musgrave's epic catalogue of Catholic treason and savagery, *Memoirs of the Different Rebellions in Ireland* (1801).

In a smaller irony, Father Patrick Fidelis Kavanagh's 'Faith and Fatherland', priests and people, *Popular History of the Insurrection of 1798* (1870) complements Musgrave's relentlessly sectarian interpretation from the opposite side of the barricade. Both books were bestsellers and went through many editions. The third edition of the *Popular History* appeared in 1884, on the eve of the Home Rule crisis, and the mass mobilisation of unionist resistance, while the fourth edition came out in the centennial year of 1898. The approach of 1898 stimulated renewed interest in 1798. Three years earlier, the poet, journalist, and Gaelic revivalist, Alice Milligan, founded the Henry Joy Literary Society in Belfast, and Bigger relaunched the *Ulster Journal of Archaeology*, which immediately attracted antiquarian contributions on Antrim and Down in '98.[16] But the centenary also stimulated unionist hostility, crisply articulated by *The Belfast News-Letter*: 'Ulster wants to forget it all, because Ulster is not proud of the rebellion, and Ulster is loyal.'[17]

All of this, of course, put liberal unionists, and provincial patriots, like the Presbyterian minister and historian, W. T. Latimer, in an awkward place – from which, in his *Ulster Biographies* (1897) he managed, rather elegantly, to extricate himself:

> It is certain that great civil and religious oppression existed in Ireland during the last century, but we must remember that measures of reform have now been granted more radical than Porter was hanged for, [and] from this fact a strong argument may be drawn for maintaining the supremacy of the imperial parliament by which these grievances have been removed.
>
> . . .
>
> Henry Joy McCracken exceeded almost every other leader of the United Irishmen in forgetfulness of self and attachment to his country

> . . . and if we as unionists condemn the fatal mistake he made, we must respect his motives, admire his courage, and venerate his memory.[18]

Latimer also records, although he does not date, the 'levelling' of graves in St George's churchyard, and the sale of the ground by the Revd Edward May, for building purposes, concluding that 'the dust of the patriot lies under one of the houses erected on this site'.[19] That was in 1897. Five years later in 1902 the builders were back, and this time struck bones, 'which from several circumstances [were] believed to be those of Henry Joy McCracken.' A local antiquarian, Robert May (no relation) took possession of the remains, which were eventually reburied in 1909 alongside those of Mary Ann, in Clifton St graveyard, abutting the old poor house built by their uncle, Robert Joy. Why May held onto them for so long is unknown (but at least, unlike the disinterred bones of Thomas Paine, they were not mislaid!) The inscription at the foot of Mary Ann's gravestone, raised by F. J. Bigger, reads *Díleas go h-éag*, which he translates as 'True till death'.[20] 'Loyal' is a stronger translation, but 'faithful' may also serve – which would have pleased Jemmy Hope.

As in R. M. Young's late nineteenth-century book, Edna Fitzhenry's 1936 biography includes the text of a 'hitherto unpublished' song, which she explains may or may not be traditional, although the use of the Scots dialect word 'dree' (endure) indicates a local provenance.[21] Neither of these songs have made their way into the modern ballad repertoire, but another one did, which begins:

An Ulsterman I am proud to be
From the Antrim Glens I come.
Although I laboured by the sea
I have followed fife and drum.

> I have heard the martial tramp of men
> I've seen them fight and die.
> It's well I do remember when
> I followed Henry Joy.

In the early 1970s Dominic Behan wrote a less well-known song, 'Our last hope', now readily accessible on YouTube, whose lyrics invoke McCracken the social radical:

> God save the Queen, God bless the Pope
> With your harps and Lambeg Drums.
> As you live in despair and die in hope
> In your Falls and your Shankill slums.
> Let's pray to God that taig and prod
> May worship each alone.
> Remember Henry Joy me friends, Bob Emmet and Wolfe Tone
> (Refrain)
>
> Let's say goodbye, my friends at last
> To bigotry and hate.
> Our future has always been the past
> No Stormont or Free State.
> Too long we've been divided friends
> Too long we've fought our own.
> Remember Henry Joy me friends . . .

The historical figure of McCracken thus resonates with left-wing republican sensibilities, and with a spirit of protestant nonconformity, ill at ease equally with Hibernian nationalism and backwoods unionism. It is easy to see, for example, why Henry Joy appealed to John Hewitt, a poet, socialist, proponent of an Ulster regional identity, and author of a play for radio, *The McCrackens*.[22]

The handwritten script of that play, which may never have been broadcast, surfaced only in the 1990s, and is characterised by Hewitt's editor as 'a pacey retort' to Jack Loudan's underwhelming *Henry Joy McCracken*, first performed in Belfast in 1945.[23] From the historian's perspective, the sub-literary quality of Loudan's effort is less interesting that the presumption that his subject commanded an audience. In 1982, in the preface to her pioneering study, *Partners in Revolution*, Marianne Elliott recalls the 'vivid repertory of United Irish plays staged by my father's amateur dramatic company, the Rosemary Theatre Group in Belfast' – Loudan's, presumably, among them.[24]

Stewart Parker's *Northern Star*, has been described as 'a protestant, but not a unionist, critique of Irish republicanism', delivered by a playwright whose politics were 'socialist and secular'.[25] Some Irish historians have been quick to criticise historical fictions for their anachronisms and factual inaccuracy; and, clearly aware of such strictures, Parker bluntly stated his 'is not an historical play'.[26] In fact it is a play written during 'the Troubles', first performed, in Belfast's Lyric Theatre, in 1984, which urgently addresses present discontents. In one exuberantly anachronistic scene towards the end, leaving the audience (or reader) in no doubt about his contemporary preoccupations, the Antrim and Down leaders rounded up in the first week of June, 1798, are subjected to interrogation as 'hooded men', an unmissable allusion to the torture of ten suspects rounded up for internment without trial in August, 1971.

The first script direction is '[*Ireland, the continuous past*]'. *Northern Star* then, does not pretend to conform to the protocols of the historian's guild but it does disclose a richly reflective and sophisticated historical imagination, and besides, Parker had clearly done his homework. Set in a ruined cottage in the Belfast mountains – where McCracken is hiding out with Mary Bodle and their daughter,

Maria – the play is composed in seven 'flashbacks', or 'ages of man', over the seven years from 1791, when the Society of United Irishmen was formed, to 1798, and the battle of Antrim. The mock-heroic, counter-romantic, tenor of the dialogue is established immediately. 'Have you ever been to Antrim. I mean it isn't exactly Paris, is it. It's scarcely Boston, it's not quite Philadelphia, is it?'[27] McCracken engages in imagined conversation with old friends and comrades, Russell, Tone, Neilson, Hope, Teeling, and Bunting, and in actual conversation with Mary, Mary Ann, and a British officer searching for rebel fugitives, and reflects on the tumultuous history of the 1790s, and on Irish history generally:

> My great-grandfather Joy was a French Huguenot, my great-grand-father McCracken was a Scottish Covenanter, persecuted, the pair of them, driven here from the shores of home, their home but not my home, because I am Henry Joy McCracken and here to stay, a natural son of Belfast, as Irish a bastard as all the other incomers, blown into this port by the storm of history. Gaelic or Danish or Anglo-Norman, without distinction, it makes no odds, every mother's son of us children of nature on this sodden glorious patch of earth, unpossessed of deed or inheritance, without distinction.[28]

And his British interlocuter is equally acute:

> The whole history of Ireland is a civil war. It was very comical of these Scotch-Presbyterian drapers and linen merchants to imagine they could make it otherwise. There has never been the least vestige of a nation-state on this island. Nor will be. There have been petty fiefdoms, Gaelic provinces, clan territories, tribal settlements – all of them in a perpetual flux of slander and slaughter. Only one allegiance has ever succeeded in uniting the majority of them – the allegiance to the British crown.[29]

Northern Star is technically inventive. Each 'flashback' is presented consecutively in a pastiche of seven great Irish dramatists, Sheridan, Boucicault, Wilde, Synge, O'Casey, Behan, and Beckett, and that chronological progression stresses the continuous contemporaneity of the still unresolved conflict of the 1790s, and the abiding relevance of Henry Joy in 1984.[30] 'Let them paint you in forty shades of green on some godforshaken gable-end!' remarks Mary Ann.[31]

Henry Joy's Volunteer uniform is preserved in the Ulster Museum and if that garment appears a surprisingly snug fit for such a tall man, we have only a story-teller's word for the 'quite authentic' provenance of McCracken's cradle, made of 'solid mahogany . . . with maple-wood inlaying', in the possession of an unnamed blacksmith.[32] The drawing after a miniature belonging to Mary Ann is the image reproduced on a plaque at the entrance to the disused Masonic Hall in Rosemary Street, Belfast, a short distance from where the McCracken family home once stood, and on a commemorative Irish postage stamp, designed by Robert Ballagh, in 1998. In 2017 a bust, also based on the drawing, was unveiled in Kilmainham Gaol, and is currently on loan to the Linenhall Library, in which Thomas Russell once served as librarian.

These artefacts and tokens of remembrance illustrate rather than explain McCracken's secure place in the imagined pantheon of Irish patriots. Dying young and on the gallows helps, but that was not precisely a select group in 1798. His charismatic and attractive personality is also germane. If Kenneth Dawson's charges of political fanaticism and murder strike a discordant note, that is because Henry Joy has otherwise received a distinctly good press, even from those, like W. T. Latimer, who rejected his politics and deplored his actions. Two further dimensions to McCracken's life and career are crucial, I think, to the making of the legend: the counterfactual force of a lost revolution, and a powerful sense of place.

The United Irish project, and its defeat, represents perhaps the most poignant and potent 'what might have been' in Irish history. If only they had got it right, if only they hadn't 'botched the birth'.[33] Henry Joy is integral to that moment, and Belfast too. Refusing Mary Ann's plea that he go to America, Parker's McCracken replies, 'I belong here. Everything I've done has been an affirmation of living here. How can I leave now?'.[34] Henry Joy McCracken's story ends, and its afterlife begins, where he was born. In Belfast.

Notes

Introduction

1 See the entry on Fitzgibbon in the *Dictionary of Irish Biography*.
2 Modern scholarship has identified the use of the term 'Protestant ascendancy' as early as 1782 but the case may still be made that, by virtue of its contemporary political impact and subsequent usage, the Dublin declaration, reiterated at the time by county grand juries across the island, remains the most important statement of that concept. W. J. McCormack, 'Eighteenth-century ascendancy: Yeats and the historians', in *Eighteenth-Century Ireland/ Iris an Dá Chultúr*, 4 (1989), pp 159–81; James Kelly, 'Eighteenth-century ascendancy: A commentary', in *Eighteenth-Century Ireland/ Iris an Dá Chultúr* 5 (1990), pp 173–87.
3 Thomas Bartlett, 'An end to moral economy: The Irish militia disturbances of 1793', in *Past & Present*, 99 (1983), pp 41–64.
4 Tom Dunne provides a detailed account of the Battle of New Ross in *Rebellions: Memoir, Memory and 1798* (Dublin, 2004, 2010).

Chapter 1

1 *Belfast News-Letter* (hereafter *BNL*), 20 July 1798.
2 Jonathan Bardon, *Belfast: An Illustrated History* (Belfast, 1982, 1983 edn), pp 3–10; McDowell, Moody, Woods (eds), *The Writings of Theobald Wolfe Tone: Volume I: Tone's Career in Ireland to June 1795* (Oxford, 1998), pp 131–2.
3 George Benn, *The History of the Town of Belfast* (Belfast, 1823), p. 3.
4 [Henry Joy], *Historical Collections Relative to the Town of Belfast* (Belfast, 1817), p. 244.
5 C. J. Woods (ed.), *Journals and Memoirs of Thomas Russell 1791–5* (Dublin, 1991), p. 150.
6 McDowell, Moody, Woods (eds), *The Writings of Theobald Wolfe Tone: Volume II: America, France, and Bantry Bay, August 1795 to December 1796* (Oxford, 2002), p. 333. See John Gray, *Cave Hill and the United Irishmen* (Belfast, 2018).
7 Revd George Hill, *An Historical Account of the Plantation in Ulster* (Belfast, 1877), p. 73.
8 A. T. Q. Stewart, *The Narrow Ground: The Roots of Conflict in Ulster* (London, 1989), p. 86.

9   In 1650 Charles II was crowned in Scotland as a covenanted king.

10 Linen Hall Library, Belfast (hereafter LHL), Joy MSS, vol iv, p.303.

11 Christopher Fox, 'Swift's Scotophobia', in *Bullán: An Irish Studies Journal* 6 (2002), pp 43–65.

12 LHL, Joy MSS, vol viii, p. 107.

13 See Ian McBride, *Scripture Politics: Ulster Presbyterianism and Irish Radicalism in the Late Eighteenth Century* (Oxford, 1998), pp 42–52.

14 For Drennan's intellectual lineage see A. T. Q. Stewart, *A Deeper Silence, the Hidden Origins of the United Irishmen* (London, 1993).

15 Mary McNeill, *The Life and Times of Mary Ann McCracken, 1770–1866: A Belfast Panorama* (1960, Belfast, 1988 edn), p. 39.

16 George Orwell, *The English People* (London, 1947), p. 12.

17 Henry Joy McCracken to Margaret and Mary Ann McCracken, 10 Jan. 1797, Public Record Office of Northern Ireland, McCracken Correspondence (copies from the R. R. Madden Papers in Trinity College, Dublin). T1218/4. 'Gasconaders' use 'boastful or bombastic language', *Oxford English Dictionary*.

18 Jacques-Louis de Bougrenet de Latocnaye, *A Frenchman's Walk Through Ireland, 1796–7* (Cork, 1798, Belfast, 1984), p. 222.

19 *BNL*, 11 Jan. 1793.

20 Hope's memoir in R. R. Madden, *Antrim and Down in '98* (Glasgow, n.d.), pp 94–5.

21 McNeill, *The Life and Times of Mary Ann McCracken*, p. 179.

Chapter 2

1   McDowell, Moody, Woods (eds), *The Writings of Theobald Wolfe Tone: Volume I: Tone's Career in Ireland to June 1795* (Oxford, 1998), pp 146-7.

2   McNeill ascribes ownership of the *Hibernia* to Henry Joy's brother Francis (*The Life and Times of Mary Ann McCracken, 1770–1866: A Belfast Panorama* (1960, Belfast, 1988 edn), p. 76), whereas McDowell et al., identify his father John as the owner (*The Writings of Theobald Wolfe Tone*, I, p. 224).

3   McDowell et al., *The Writings of Theobald Wolfe Tone*, I, p. 146.

4   McNeill, *Mary Ann McCracken*, p. 151.

5   Jean Agnew, *Belfast Merchant Families in the Seventeenth Century* (Dublin, 1996), p. 20.

6   Ibid., pp 14–15.

7   Ibid., p. 42.

8   [Henry Joy], *Historical Collections Relative to the Town of Belfast* (Belfast, 1817), pp 83–4.

9   Edna C. Fitzhenry, *Henry Joy McCracken* (Dublin, 1936), p. 23; C. J. Woods, 'Francis Joy', in the *Dictionary of Irish Biography*.

10 *Belfast News-Letter* (hereafter *BNL*), 30 Dec. 1774.

11 Fitzhenry, *Henry Joy McCracken*, p. 22.

12 There is a copy of this lecture in the author's own hand, in Linen Hall Library, Belfast (hereafter LHL), Joy MSS, vol. xiii.

13 S. J. Connolly, 'Improving town, 1750–1820', in S. J. Connolly (ed.), *Belfast 400: People, Place, and History* (Liverpool, 2012), p. 162.

14 LHL, Joy MSS, vol. vi, 190.

15 Connolly, 'Improving town', p. 173.

16 [Henry Joy], *Historical Collections*, p. 110, p. 117, pp 244–5.

17 Local interest in American affairs is indicated by an advertisement placed in the *News-Letter* by John Hays, bookseller and stationer, 'at the TWO BIBLES, in Bridge Street', offering for sale Anderson's pills, stamped paper, bonds and 'The map of Boston at 1s 1d, the same coloured at 1s 7d', in *Belfast News-Letter* 29 Sept. 1775.

18 Richard K. McMaster, *Scots-Irish Merchants in Colonial America: The Flaxseed Trade and Emigration from Ireland, 1718–1775* (Belfast, 2009), p. 252. McMaster gives 9000 as the most up-to-date figure for emigrants in 1773. Most other estimates are higher. 'Redemptioners' were indentured to work off the cost of their passage in America.

19 *BNL*, 3 Jan. 1775.

20 [Henry Joy], *Historical Collections Relative to the Town of Belfast*, p. 118.

21 McNeill, *Mary Ann McCracken*, pp 30–1.

22 McDowell, Moody, Woods (eds), *The Writings of Theobald Wolfe Tone: Volume II: America, France and Bantry Bay, August 1795 to December 1796* (Oxford, 2002), p. 284.

23 See Padhraig Higgins, *A Nation of Politicians: Gender, Patriotism, and Political Culture in Late Eighteenth-Century Ireland* (Madison, 2010).

24 McNeill, *Mary Ann McCracken*, p. 34.

25 R. R. Madden, *Antrim and Down in '98*, (Glasgow, n.d.), p. 8.

26 Henry Joy McCracken to Mary Ann McCracken, 12 May 1798, Public Record Office of Northern Ireland, McCracken Correspondence T1218/41

27 Castlereagh's pass, for Henry and Mrs Joy, dated 9 June 1798, LHL, Joy MSS vol. ix, f.18.

Chapter 3

1 Cathal O'Byrne, 'The cradle of a '98 hero' in *As I Roved Out: A Book of the North: Being a Series of Historical Sketches of Ulster and Old Belfast* (Belfast, 1946, facsimile edn, 1982), p. 205.

2 Mary McNeill, *The Life and Times of Mary Ann McCracken, 1770–1866: A Belfast Panorama* (1960, Belfast, 1988 edn), pp 117–18.

3 Edna C. Fitzhenry, *Henry Joy McCracken* (Dublin, 1936), p. 40, p. 96.

4 Hope described McCracken as 'by far the most deserving of all our northern leaders', R. R. Madden, *Antrim and Down in '98*, (Glasgow, n.d.), p. 106.

5 Fitzhenry, *Henry Joy McCracken*, p. 25, p. 29.

6 McNeill, *Mary Ann McCracken*, p. 139.

7 McDowell, Moody, Woods (eds), *The Writings of Theobald Wolfe Tone: Volume I: Tone's Career in Ireland to June 1795* (Oxford, 1998), p. 30, p. 112, p. 115, p. 174.

8 Fitzhenry, *Henry Joy McCracken*, p. 52; Cathal O'Byrne attributes that argument to Mary Ann, 'The cradle of a '98 hero', in *As I Roved Out: A Book of the North, Being a Series of Historical Sketches of Ulster and Old Belfast* (Belfast, 1946)., p. 207.

9 Fitzhenry, *Henry Joy McCracken*, pp 40–1.

10 [Henry Joy], *Historical Collections Relative to the Town of Belfast* (Belfast, 1817), p. 242.

11 David Dickson, 'Paine and Ireland' in Dickson, Keogh, Whelan (eds), *The United Irishmen: Republicanism, Radicalism and Rebellion* (Dublin, 1993), pp 135–50; McDowell et al., *The Writings of Theobald Wolfe Tone, I*, pp 131–2.

12 John Keogh to (Bishop Thomas Mussey), 2 Oct. 1792. Public Record Office (Kew) HO 100/38/275. Quoted in Jim Smyth, *The Men of No Property: Irish Radicals and Popular Politics in the Late Eighteenth Century* (London, 1992), p. 65.

13 McDowell et al., *The Writings of Theobald Wolfe Tone, I*, p. 128.

14 Belfast Central Library, Bigger Collection, K11/2.

15 Tone referred to this group as the 'time to time party': McDowell et al., *The Writings of Theobald Wolfe Tone, I*, p. 209.

16 R. B. McDowell, 'The personnel of the Dublin Society of United Irishmen, 1791–4', in *Irish Historical Studies*, ii:5 (1940) pp 12–53.

17 *National Evening Star*, 5, 7, 10, 14 Dec. 1792.

18 McDowell et al., *The Writings of Theobald Wolfe Tone, I*, p. 398.

19 The phrase is A. P. W. Malcomson's, *John Foster: The Politics of the Anglo-Irish Ascendancy* (Oxford, 1978), p. 409.

20 Thomas Bartlett, 'An end to moral economy: The Irish militia disturbances of 1793', in *Past & Present*, 99, (1983) pp 41–64.

21 Martha McTier to William Drennan, n.d. March, 1 Apr. 1793, Jean Agnew (ed.), *The Drennan–McTier Letters*, i (Dublin, 1998), p. 502, p. 509; [Henry Joy], *Historical Collections*, p. 416.

22 Samuel McTier to Martha McTier and Drennan, 22 and 24 Apr. 1793, Agnew (ed.), *The Drennan–McTier Letters*, i, p. 518, p. 523.

23 James Kelly, *'That Damn'd Thing Called Honour': Duelling in Ireland, 1570–1860* (Cork, 1995), pp 133–4; McDowell, Moody, Woods (eds), *The Writings of Theobald Wolfe Tone: Volume III: France, The Rhine, Lough Swilly and Death of Tone, January 1797 to November 1798* (Oxford, 2007), p. 212.

24 George Benn, *The History of the Town of Belfast* (Belfast, 1823), p. 61.

25 McTier to Drennan, 1 Apr. 1793, Agnew (ed.), *Drennan–McTier Letters*, p. 509.

26 Samuel McTier to Martha McTier and Drennan, 24 Apr. 1793 Agnew (ed.), in *Drennan–McTier Letters*, p. 523.

Chapter 4

1 McDowell, Moody, Woods (eds), *The Writings of Theobald Wolfe Tone: Volume I: Tone's Career in Ireland to June 1795* (Oxford, 1998), p. 104, p. 448.

2 On the sustained centrality of Neilson to the entire United Irish project see Kenneth L. Dawson, *The Belfast Jacobin: Samuel Neilson and the United Irishmen* (Dublin, 2017).

3 McDowell, Moody, Woods (eds), *The Writings of Theobald Wolfe Tone: Volume II: America, France, and Bantry Bay, August 1795 to December 1796* (Oxford, 2002), p. 333.

4 R. R. Madden, *Antrim and Down in '98* (Glasgow, n.d.), p. 13.

5 McDowell et al., *The Writings of Theobald Wolfe Tone, I,* pp 183–5; Thomas Russell, *A Letter to the People of Ireland on the Present Situation in the Country* (Belfast, 1796), reprinted in H. T. Dickinson, *Ireland in the Age of Revolution, 1760–1805* (London, 2013), iv, pp 394–7.

6 *Northern Star,* 18 July 1796.

7 *Belfast News-Letter,* 3 Oct. 1774, italics added.

8 C. J. Woods (ed.), *Journals and Memoirs of Thomas Russell, 1791–5* (Dublin, 1991), pp 66–7.

9 Andrew Fletcher, *An Account of a Conversation Concerning a Right Regulation of Governments for the Common Good of Mankind* (London, 1703), p. 10.

10 *Paddy's Resource: Being a Select Collection of Original and Modern Patriotic Songs Compiled for the Use of the People of Ireland* (Dublin [New York?], 1798), p. 57.

11 Ibid., p. 92.

12 Edna C. Fitzhenry, *Henry Joy McCracken* (Dublin, 1936), p. 37; Harry White, 'Bunting, Edward', in the *Dictionary of Irish Biography*.

13 McDowell et al., *The Writings of Theobald Wolfe Tone, I,* pp 212–13.

14 Russell, *A Letter to the People of Ireland,* p. 312.

15 'The children's catechism', Linen Hall Library, Belfast, Joy MSS, vol viii.

16 Thomas Bartlett, 'Select documents XXXVIII: Defenders and defenderism in 1795', in *Irish Historical Studies* 24:95 (1985), pp 373–94.

17 Edward Cooke to Thomas Pelham, 5 Dec. 1795, Public Record Office of Northern Ireland (hereafter PRONI), Pelham Transcripts, T 755/2; for Maginnis, and for masonry in general, see Petri Mirala, *Freemasonry in Ulster, 1733–1813: A Social and Political History of the Masonic Brotherhood in the North of Ireland* (Dublin, 2007).

18 General John Knox to Edward Cooke, 5 June 1798. National Archives of Ireland, Rebellion Papers, 620/38/61.

19 Henry Joy McCracken to Mary Ann, 18 June 1798, PRONI, McCracken Correspondence, T1218/42.

Chapter 5

1 The United Irishmen invested much time and effort in attempting to suborn militiamen; Kenneth Dawson thus speculates that Neilson joined the Lisburn lodge with an eye to the nearby Blaris militia camp. Dawson, *The Belfast Jacobin: Samuel Neilson and the United Irishmen* (Dublin, 2017) p. 91.

2 McDowell, Moody, Woods (eds), *The Writings of Theobald Wolfe Tone: Volume II: America, France, and Bantry Bay, August 1795 to December 1796* (Oxford, 2002), p. 16, p. 334.

3 Ibid., p. 22.

4 R. R. Madden, *Antrim and Down in '98* (Glasgow, n.d.), p. 14.

5 Dawson, *The Belfast Jacobin,* p. 82.

6 Dawson, 'Henry Joy McCracken: Rebel hero, and a man not afraid to murder', in *Belfast Telegraph,* 8 July 2015.

7   Mary McNeill, *The Life and Times of Mary Ann McCracken, 1770–1866: A Belfast Panorama* (1960, Belfast, 1988 edn), p. 142.

8   [Henry Joy], *Historical Collections Relative to the Town of Belfast* (Belfast, 1817), pp 436–7; Madden, *Antrim and Down in '98*, pp 112–13.

9   Charles Hamilton Teeling, *History of the Irish Rebellion of 1798: A Personal Narrative* (London, 1828, Glasgow, 1876 edn), p. 12.

10   James Quinn, *Soul on Fire: A Life of Thomas Russell* (Dublin, 2002), p. 97.

11   Dawson, *Belfast Jacobin*, p. 87.

12   William Godwin, *Things as They Are; or The Adventures of Caleb Williams* (London, 1988 Penguin edn), p. 184.

13   Teeling, *History of the Irish Rebellion*, pp 21–2.

14   Michael Ignatieff, *A Just Measure of Pain: The Penitentiary in the Industrial Revolution, 1750–1850* (London, 1978, 1989), p. 16.

15   Brian Henry, *Dublin Hanged: Crime, Law Enforcement, and Punishment in Late Eighteenth-Century Dublin* (Dublin, 1994), p. 100.

16   Quoted in Ignatieff, *A Just Measure of Pain*, p. 52.

17   Godwin, *Caleb Williams*, p. 187, p. 191; Teeling, *History of the Irish Rebellion*, p. 23, p. 27.

18   Henry Joy McCracken to Margaret and Mary Ann, 27 June 1797, Public Record Office of Northern Ireland (hereafter PRONI), McCracken Correspondence, T1218/20.

19   Ibid., 10 Jan.,1797, PRONI, McCracken Correspondence, T1218/4.

20   Teeling, *History of the Irish Rebellion*, pp 24–5, pp 28–9.

21   Ibid., p. 25.

22   Henry Joy McCracken to Mary Ann 3 Aug. 1797, PRONI, McCracken Correspondence, T1218/25.

23   Henry Joy McCracken to Mary Ann, 1 Sept. 1797, PRONI, McCracken Correspondence, T1218/28.

24   McDowell, Moody, Woods (eds), *The Writings of Theobald Wolfe Tone: Volume III: France, The Rhine, Lough Swilly and Death of Tone, January 1797 to November 1798* (Oxford, 2007), p. 477.

25   Mary Ann McCracken to Henry Joy McCracken, 16 Mar. 1797, Henry Joy to Mary Ann, 28 Apr. 1797, PRONI, McCracken Correspondence, T1218/7, 12.

26   Edna C. Fitzhenry, *Henry Joy McCracken* (Dublin, 1936), pp 98–9.

27   Teeling, *History of the Irish Rebellion*, p. 30; Sean Connolly, *Divided Kingdom: Ireland, 1630–1800* (Oxford, 2008), p. 475.

28   McNeill, *Life of Mary Ann McCracken*, p. 124.

Chapter 6

1   I discuss these apologetics in Jim Smyth, 'Who fears to speak of '99?', in *Dublin Review of Books* 57 (2014).

2   Henry Joy McCracken to Mary Ann, 12 May 1798, Public Record Office of Northern Ireland (hereafter PRONI), McCracken Correspondence, T1218/41.

3   It is not clear if Jemmy Hope included Simms in his scathing indictment of the 'foreign aid' renegades who flinched when the moment of decision

arrived; however, in a poignant footnote R. R. Madden, who valorised Hope, reveals that in 1842 the 81-year-old Simms declined to be interviewed, *Antrim and Down in '98* (Glasgow, n.d.), p. 123n.

4 Thomas Bartlett, 'Defence, counter-insurgency, and rebellion: Ireland, 1793–1803', in Bartlett and Jeffrey (eds), *A Military History of Ireland* (Cambridge, 1996), p. 281.

5 *The Manuscripts and Correspondence of James, First Earl of Charlemont* (Historical Manuscripts Commission, London, 1894), ii, p. 324.

6 Madden, *Antrim and Down in '98*, p. 105.

7 Edna C. Fitzhenry, *Henry Joy McCracken* (Dublin, 1936), p. 113.

8 Linen Hall Library, Belfast, Joy MSS iv, p. 328; Mary McNeill, *The Life and Times of Mary Ann McCracken, 1770–1866: A Belfast Panorama* (1960, Belfast, 1988 edn), p. 174

9 [Henry Joy], *Historical Collections Relative to the Town of Belfast* (Belfast, 1817), pp 480–2.

10 Madden, *Antrim and Down in '98*, pp 45–6.

11 Hudson to Charlemont, 18 July, 27 July 1798, *Charlemont MSS*, ii, pp 327–8. For skilful historical reconstructions of the Battle of Antrim see Charles Dickson, *Revolt in the North: Antrim and Down in 1798* (London, 1960), and A. T. Q. Stewart, *The Summer Soldiers: The 1798 Rebellion in Antrim and Down* (Belfast, 1995).

12 Charles Hamilton Teeling, *History of the Irish Rebellion of 1798: A Personal Narrative* (London, 1828, Glasgow, 1876 edn), p. 124; Madden, *Antrim and Down in '98*, p. 123.

13 Hudson indicates that some Defenders were 'out': 'a schism was apprehended with Defenders … that they had leaders of a higher description than those who appeared I well know'. Hudson to Charlemont, 18 July 1798, *Charlemont MSS*, ii, p. 327.

14 Account of the Battle of Antrim by the Revd Dr McCarthy, magistrate, in Madden, *Antrim and Down in '98*, p. 55.

15 Hudson to Charlemont, 17 June 1798, *Charlemont MSS*, ii, p. 324.

16 Ibid.; Teeling, *History of the Irish Rebellion*, p. 125.

17 Henry George Purdon, *Memoirs of Service of the 64th Regiment, Second Straffordshire: 1758 to 1881* (London, 1891) pp 33–4.

18 Madden, *Antrim and Down in '98*, p. 49.

19 Teeling, *History of the Irish Rebellion*, p. 127; *Charlemont MSS*, ii, p. 328.

20 Samuel McSkimin, *Annals of Ulster, or Ireland Fifty Years Ago* (Belfast, 1849, 1906 edn), p. 81 and editor, E. J. Crum's note, p. 104.

21 *BNL*, 8 June 1798.

22 James Orr, 'Donegore Hill' (1804), The Scots word 'Skail' translates as 'a spill or scattering'.

23 William Fox, 'A narrative of the proceedings of the Republican Army of the county Down during the late insurrection', quoted by Bartlett, in *Military History of Ireland*, p. 282.

24 Teeling, *History of the Irish Rebellion*, p. 127.

Chapter 7

1 Charles Hamilton Teeling, *History of the Irish Rebellion of 1798: A Personal Narrative* (London, 1828, Glasgow, 1876 edn), p. 127–8; Clavering named Robert Johnstone, William Orr and the brothers Samuel and John Orr, but not McCracken, Fred Heatley, *Henry Joy McCracken and His Times* (Belfast, 1967), p. 39.

2 R. R. Madden, *Antrim and Down in '98* (Glasgow, n.d.), pp 51–2.

3 [Henry Joy], *Historical Collections Relative to the Town of Belfast* (Belfast, 1817), x; *Belfast News-Letter*, 15 June 1798.

4 Henry Joy McCracken to Mary Ann 18 June 1798, Public Records Office of Northern Ireland (hereafter PRONI), McCracken Correspondence, T1218/42.

5 Charles Hamilton Teeling, *History of the Irish Rebellion of 1798: A Personal Narrative* (London, 1828, Glasgow, 1876 edn), p. 43; see also Thomas Bartlett, 'Informers, informants and information: the secret history of the 1790s reconsidered', in Bartlett, Dickson, Keogh and Whelan (eds), *1798: A Bicentenary Perspective* (Dublin, 2003).

6 Madden, *Antrim and Down in '98*, p. 40, p. 46.

7 Ibid., p. 104.

8 Mary McNeill, *The Life and Times of Mary Ann McCracken, 1770–1866: A Belfast Panorama* (1960, Belfast, 1988 edn), p. 179.

9 Stewart Parker, *Northern Star*, in Parker, *Three Plays for Ireland* (Birmingham, 1989), p. 36. In this edition, as in every subsequent production, the subtitle is deleted.

10 Edward Young, *Selected Poems*, introduced by Brian Hepworth (Cheshire, 1975).

11 The verdict of Parker's McCracken is that 'Night Thoughts' is 'a better sedative than whiskey', Parker, *Northern Star*, p. 42.

12 C. J. Woods (ed.), *Journals and Memoirs of Thomas Russell 1791–5* (Dublin, 1991), p. 123.

13 Henry Joy McCracken to Mary Ann, 19 Nov. 1797, PRONI, McCracken Correspondence, T1218/35; Madden, *Antrim and Down in '98*, p. 104.

14 *Belfast News-Letter*, 10 July 1798.

15 McNeill, *Mary Ann McCracken*, p. 180.

16 Ibid., p. 182; Martha McTier to William Drennan, 18 Oct. 1798, Jean Agnew (ed.), *The Drennan–McTier Letters*, ii (Dublin, 1998), p. 417.

17 McNeill, *Mary Ann McCracken*, p. 184.

18 Edna C. Fitzhenry, *Henry Joy McCracken* (Dublin, 1936), p. 150.

19 McNeill, *Mary Ann McCracken*, p. 185.

20 W. J. Bate and Albrecht Strauss (eds), *The Yale Edition of the Works of Samuel Johnson* (New Haven and London, 1969), p. 242; E. P. Thompson, *Whigs and Hunters: The Origin of the Black Act* (London, 1975); Peter Linebaugh, *The London Hanged: Crime and Civil Society in the Eighteenth Century* (second edn, London, 2006), and Michel Foucault, *Discipline and Punish* (London, 1977), trans. Alan Sheridan.

21 McDowell, Moody, Woods (eds), *The Writings of Theobald Wolfe Tone: Volume III: France, The Rhine, Lough Swilly and Death of Tone, January 1797 to November 1798* (Oxford, 2007), p. 368.

22 Brian Henry, *Dublin Hanged: Crime, Law Enforcement, and Punishment in Late Eighteenth-Century Dublin* (Dublin, 1994), p. 16.

23 Linebaugh, *London Hanged*, p. xxii.

24 Bate and Strauss (eds), *The Works of Samuel Johnson*, p. 244.

25 J. Bennett Nolen (ed.), *Benjamin Franklin in Scotland and Ireland: 1759 and 1771* (Philadelphia, 1938, 1956 edn), p. 33.

26 Charles Dickson, *Revolt in the North: Antrim and Down in 1798* (London, 1960), pp 250–1.

27 Statement of Patrick Scott, Belfast Central Library, Bigger Collection, K11/31.

28 [Henry Joy], *Historical Collections*, pp 489–91.

29 McDowell, Moody, Woods (eds), *The Writings of Theobald Wolfe Tone: Volume II: America, France, and Bantry Bay, August 1795 to December 1796* (Oxford, 2002), pp 106–7.

30 Woods (ed.), *Thomas Russell 1791–5* (Dublin, 1991), p. 123.

31 Fitzhenry, *Henry Joy McCracken*, p. 65.

32 *The Writings of Theobald Wolfe Tone*, iii, p. 359.

33 James Quinn, *Soul on Fire: A Life of Thomas Russell* (Dublin, 2002), p. 297.

34 Teeling, *History of the Irish Rebellion*, p. 129.

35 McTier to Drennan, 31 May 1798, Jean Agnew (ed.), *The Drennan–McTier Letters*, ii (Dublin, 1998), p. 409. Nugent did, however, display conspicuous ruthlessness against the rebels after the Battle of Ballinahinch.

36 Madden, *Antrim and Down in '98*, p. 127.

Chapter 8

1 Rory Fitzpatrick, *God's Frontiersmen: The Scots–Irish Epic* (London, 1989), p. 14; Stewart Parker, *Northern Star*, in *Three Plays for Ireland* (Birmingham, 1989), p. 64; McBride, 'Memory and forgetting: Ulster Presbyterians and 1798', in Bartlett, Dickson, Keogh and Whelan (eds), *1798: A Bicentenary Perspective* (Dublin, 2003), p. 479.

2 Fred Heatley, *Henry Joy McCracken and His Times* (Belfast, 1967), p. 45.

3 [Henry Joy], *Historical Collections Relative to the Town of Belfast* (Belfast, 1817), p. 492.

4 Bartlett, 'Clemency and compensation: The treatment of defeated rebels and suffering loyalists after the 1798 rebellion', in J Smyth, (ed.), *Revolution, Counter-Revolution and Union, Ireland in the 1790s* (Cambridge, 2001).

5 Edna C. Fitzhenry, *Henry Joy McCracken* (Dublin, 1936), pp 150–2.

6 Mary Ann McCracken, to Henry Joy, 16 March, Apr. 1797, Public Records Office of Northern Ireland, McCracken Correspondence, T1218/7.

7 Glenn Patterson *The Mill for Grinding Old People Young* (London, 2012), p. 19.

8 The McCracken letters and the original of Hope's memoir are preserved in the Madden Papers in Trinity College, Dublin.

9 Samuel McSkimin, *Annals of Ulster, or Ireland Fifty Years Ago* (Belfast, 1849, 1906 edn), p. 89.

10 Quoted in Guy Beiner, 'Disremembering 1798? An Archaeology of Social Forgetting and Remembrance in Ulster', in *History and Memory*. 25:1 (2013), p. 22.

11 Seamus Heaney, 'Whatever You Say, Say Nothing'.

12 Revd Steel Dickson, *Narrative of Confinement and Exile* (Dublin, 1812), p. 51.

13 Charles Hamilton Teeling, *History of the Irish Rebellion of 1798: A Personal Narrative* (London, 1828, Glasgow, 1876 edn), p. 123, p. 129.

14 Belfast Central Library, Bigger Collection, K7/5/24.

15 R. M. Young, *Ulster in '98: Episodes and Anecdotes* (Belfast, 1893), pp 52–4. The reliability of Burn's memory is, however, cast into question by his 'recollection' that Henry Joy did not take part in the Battle of Antrim but had been outside the town with Samuel Orr and 15,000 men (presumably being held in reserve).

16 McBride, 'Memory and forgetting', p. 492.

17 Quoted in Beiner, 'Disremembering 1798?', p. 10.

18 W. T. Latimer, *Ulster Biographies: Relating Chiefly to the Rebellion of 1798* (Belfast, 1897), 'To the reader', v, p. 20.

19 Ibid., p. 20.

20 F. J. Bigger, 'Memorials of the patriot dead: MacCorly, Dickson, MacCracken', in *Ulster Journal of Archaeology*, 15:2 (1909), pp 93–5.

21 Fitzhenry, pp 158–9. Heatley notes that this song has been attributed to both William Drennan and P. J. McCall, *Henry Joy McCracken*, p. 57.

22 John Hewitt, edited with and introduction by Damian Smyth, *Two Plays: The McCrackens; The Angry Dove* (Belfast, 1999).

23 The Irish Theatre Institute gives 31 Mar. 1945 as the date of first production, in the Group Theatre, Belfast. http://www.irishplayography.com/play.aspx?playid=31205

24 Marianne Elliott, *Partners in Revolution: The United Irishmen and France* (New Haven, 1982), p. ix.

25 Marilynn Richtarik, *Stewart Parker: A life* (Oxford, 2012), p. 253, p. 56.

26 Ibid., p. 269. Mysteriously, the historically tendentious (even preposterous) novels of Roddy Doyle and Sebastian Barry have been spared such tetchy rebuke.

27 Parker, *Northern Star*, p. 17.

28 Ibid.

29 Ibid., p. 47.

30 Ibid.

31 Ibid., p. 54. The references to wall murals and to Johnny Cash's song 'Forty Shades Green' are good examples of Parker's use of deliberate anachronism.

32 Cathal O'Byrne, 'The cradle of a '98 hero', in *As I Roved Out: A Book of the North: Being a Series of Historical Sketches of Ulster and Old Belfast* (Belfast, 1946, facsimile edn, 1982), p. 205.

33 Parker, *Northern Star*, p. 75.

34 Ibid., p. 53.

Select Bibliography

The name of Henry Joy McCracken features more brightly in popular tradition, or 'social memory', than in more formal historical accounts of Ireland in the 1790s. The comparative lightness of his footprint in the received narrative does not accurately reflect his political weight in the councils of the United Irishmen; it is rather a function of the relatively scanty amount of 'evidence' about his thoughts and doings that he left behind. Some correspondence survives, to be sure, but nothing to compare to, for example, Theobald Wolfe Tone's or Dr William Drennan's letters, journals, and pamphlets. Yet he is among the most well-remembered of that celebrated generation. Justly so, as this book argues.

To begin with the wider historical contexts: Henry Joy's politics were forged in eighteenth-century Belfast. For that period generally see Ian McBride, *Eighteenth-Century Ireland: The Isle of Slaves* (Dublin, 2009), and for the town, S. J. Connolly (ed.), *Belfast 400: People, Place, and History* (Liverpool, 2012). A. T. Q. Stewart, *A Deeper Silence: The Hidden Origins of the United Irishmen* (London, 1993; Belfast, 1998), elaborates the social, religious and intellectual, roots of the world that made Drennan – and McCracken. Today the 1790s is the object of a rich and expanding historical literature, too voluminous to itemise here, but the scale and depth of modern scholarship on the revolutionary decade is most readily sampled in Thomas Bartlett, David Dickson, Dáire Keogh, and Kevin Whelan, (eds), *1798: A Bicentenary Perspective* (Dublin, 2003). A. T. Q. Stewart, *The Summer Soldiers: The 1798 Rebellion in Antrim and Down* (Belfast, 1995) tells the story of the battle of Antrim with signature brio, while Guy Beiner, *Forgetful Remembrance: Social Forgetting and Vernacular Historiography of a Rebellion in Ulster* (Oxford, 2018) tracks the retellings of 'the turn out' down the generations with stringent theoretical sophistication.

A number of recent biographies of his closest associates get closer to McCracken specifically: Kenneth Dawson, *The Belfast Jacobin: Samuel Neilson and the United Irishmen* (Newbridge, 2013). James Quinn, *Soul on Fire: A Life of*

Thomas Russell, 1767–1803 (Dublin, 2002) and Marianne Elliott, *Wolfe Tone* (Liverpool, 2nd edn 2012). Versions of the past are forever changing, and every generation requires its 'updated' interpretation of Tone. Ultan Gillen's is forthcoming, but as intellectual preoccupations and fashions inevitably evolve, R. B. McDowell, T. W. Moody, and C. J. Woods, (eds), *The Writings of Theobald Wolfe Tone 1763–1798*. 3 vols (Oxford, 1998–2007) will remain the scholarly bedrock.

Probably for the reasons suggested above McCracken himself has not yet received full-dress biographical treatment. The best most detailed account is still to be found in Mary McNeill, *The Life and Times of Mary Ann McCracken, 1770–1866: A Belfast Panorama* (Belfast, 1960, 1988, 2019). Edna C. Fitzhenry, *Henry Joy McCracken* (Dublin, 1936), and Fred Heatley, *Henry Joy McCracken and His Times* (Belfast, 1967), are serviceable. All three are notable for the palpable esteem of the authors for (or partisanship towards) their subject. Heatley was an early activist in the Northern civil rights movement, whose pamphlet was published in association with the Wolfe Tone Clubs. All three testify too, to the contemporary appeal and resonance of the figure of McCracken in what Stewart Parker in his 1984 play, *Northern Star*, called 'the continuous past'.

Index